Etienne Bannelier

Direct and indirect players in the fight against money laundering

Etienne Bannelier

Direct and indirect players in the fight against money laundering

The example of the French system for combating money laundering

TABLE OF CONTENTS:

For many years, money laundering cases have fuelled the imagination and curiosity of the entire world. From the illicit activities of mafia families implicating senior public or private officials to political and financial scandals, the list of cases is long, but the public's interest in such stories worthy of the best gangster films remains the same. And yet these cases are very real and sometimes manage to catch up with, or even surpass, fiction.

Numerous international investigations have uncovered ultra-sophisticated money laundering circuits, organised on a global scale and involving people who could legitimately be considered above suspicion, reflecting the need for criminal organisations to create ever more sophisticated schemes in order to evade increasingly sophisticated regulations.

Like the *piovra, the* symbol of the Italian Mafia, these networks have numerous 'tentacles' throughout the world which, even when severed, grow back to reappear elsewhere, posing a real problem for the organisations responsible for combating such money-laundering activities.

But before getting to the heart of the matter, we need to look at the real concept of money laundering. What is it? What does it cover and how is it implemented?

§1 The concept of money laundering

A general, international definition comes from the FATF[1] and states that *"many criminal acts aim to generate profits for the individual or group that commits them. Money laundering thus consists of reprocessing these proceeds of criminal origin to disguise their illegal origin (...) and is of essential importance since it enables the criminal to benefit from these profits while protecting their source".* [2]

Numerous international investigations have revealed the colossal sums that can be generated by these various underground activities, such as the illegal sale of arms, smuggling and drug trafficking. The interest shown by the various criminal organisations in setting up sophisticated networks is justified by their desire to "legitimise" these illegally acquired gains.

However, the inclusion of this offence in national legislation is based on a more precise definition. For example, the definition provided by the French legislator in Article 324-1 of the Criminal Code states that *"Money laundering is the act of facilitating, by any means, the false justification of the origin of the assets or income*

---

[1] Groupe d'Action Financière or Financial Action Task Force (FATF) is an intergovernmental body for combating money laundering and the financing of terrorism (see P. 16 below).
[2] **Money laundering: what is it?** *FATF Press Release*

of the perpetrator of a crime or offence that has procured him a direct or indirect profit.

Money laundering also includes assisting in the investment, concealment or conversion of the direct or indirect proceeds of a crime or offence.

Although this definition is limited in scope because it is national (money laundering is most often organised at an international level), it highlights the necessary precondition for this provision: the existence of an underlying offence or crime.

The prosecution must prove two things: that a criminally reprehensible act has been committed that has directly or indirectly benefited the perpetrator, and that schemes have been used to justify or conceal the origin of the funds or assets acquired in this way. It is therefore easy to understand why investigations into these transactions only come to fruition after many years.

The desire to set up ingenious money laundering schemes of this kind is not new, and has been around since the emergence of the first Sicilian Mafia families. The very origin of the practice of money laundering is not clearly determined. What's more, the term *money laundering* is relatively recent, although historians have different versions of how it originated.

Some of them attribute its origin to the Italian-American mafia practice of washing new counterfeit notes that the criminals intended to reintroduce onto the market to give them a worn appearance.[3] Furthermore, although the practice of placing counterfeit notes on the market was already a federal offence, the reintroduction of illegally collected sums was still very marginal.

Another theory on the origin of the expression, although considered fanciful but contributing greatly to the 'legend' of the practice, is that in the 1920s a Mafia family bought a chain of laundries in Chicago, the *Sanitary Cleaning Shops*, with a view to disguising the profits from their many illicit activities behind a legal façade[4].

However, whatever the origin of the term *"money laundering"*, many Mafiosi in the first half of the 20th century, particularly Lucky Luciano and his associate Meyer Lansky[5], quickly understood the need to develop increasingly complex money laundering techniques, particularly through island states.

It should also be pointed out that the practice of laundering tax fraud, as we hear so much about it in the media[6], is a special case of money laundering. In fact, the

---

[3] *La problématique du blanchiment, p.3*, Michel Koutouzis, Jean-François Thony, "Le blanchiment", 2005, Presses Universitaires de France

[4] Genesis of the money laundering process, MANOUK V., Revue Internationale de Criminologie et de Police Technique et Scientifique (RICPTS)

[5] *Lucky Luciano* (1897 - 1962) and *Meyer Lansky* (1902 - 1983) are most often considered by historians to be the main "founders" of modern organised crime.

[6] The *SwissLeaks* affair in February 2015, which affected HSBC's Swiss subsidiary, and the *Panama Papers* in 2016 are

laundering of tax fraud[7] is defined, in short, as the act of "reinjecting" the money from tax fraud into the legal economic and monetary circuit with a view to laundering it, in the same way as traditional money laundering. Initially, therefore, the laundering of tax fraud is not necessarily linked to criminal activity and is therefore the result of a simple tax offence. However, the laundering of tax fraud can be combined with the laundering of the proceeds of criminal activity[8] .

§2 The stages of money laundering

Traditionally, a money laundering operation is carried out in three stages, which may be carried out successively or sometimes simultaneously. This classification is the result of numerous international investigations, relayed by FATF communications[9] , although the translation of the terms from English to French is not very precise. In any case, this classification is not binding, but it is a constant in the various international money laundering processes, providing a better understanding of the phenomenon. The first of these is **placement** *(placement stage), during which* "dirty" money is reintroduced into the legal economic system in order to disguise its illicit origin. For example, if a business generates large amounts of cash, it quickly becomes necessary to convert these funds into higher-value banknotes, cheques or any other financial instrument (foreign currency, bearer bonds, etc.) or even in the form of goods that can be traded as a monetary instrument (gold, diamonds), as the weight of accumulated profits quickly becomes cumbersome. This investment phase can also be carried out through businesses with a reputation for handling large amounts of cash, such as restaurants, hotels, casinos, etc. The money reinjected in this way is mixed with the legal income of the shell company and sent to the bank, which is unable to detect the fraudulent origin of these sums as it has no knowledge of the exact accounts of the business concerned.

However, this *placement is* the most delicate stage for money launderers and the easiest for investigators to detect, especially with the introduction of increasingly stringent regulations, particularly in terms of detection: identification of depositing customers, declaration of suspicion by banks on certain transfers, etc.

In response to these measures aimed at detecting dirty money, criminal organisations are looking for new payment techniques such as bartering (weapons for precious

---

some of the biggest recent scandals involving tax fraud laundering.

[7] Tax fraud laundering is not covered by a specific criminal provision, but is based on a combination of article 324-1 of the French Criminal Code, which deals with money laundering, and article 1741 of the French General Tax Code, which deals with tax fraud.

[8] Many criminals combine these two types of money laundering. This was the case of Al Capone, who was imprisoned on 5 June 1931 for tax fraud.

[9] **How is money laundered?** *FATF Press Release*

stones or drugs) in order to avoid the exchange of cash that might attract the attention of the authorities.

Another technique contributing to the investment stage is the cash purchase of negotiable goods from persons not subject to the same legal obligations as credit institutions. The purchase of foreign currency from bureaux de change, luxury goods or antiques in the name of a third party, or the acquisition of gold and precious stones (whose universal monetary value is a panacea for criminal organisations) are all operations that enable money launderers to dispose of their large amounts of cash as discreetly as possible.

This is followed by the second phase of the money laundering process, **the** *layering stage,* during which the launderer accumulates numerous complex financial transactions with the aim of reducing the traceability of the reinjected funds and, as a result, distancing them from their source, in this case the launderer himself.

These operations are carried out to blend directly into the multitude of legitimate transactions involving millions of dollars carried out every day.

Faced with the measures put in place to combat money laundering, particularly with banks and tax havens, criminal organisations are increasingly forced to turn to new investment and stacking techniques.

But the imagination of money launderers knows no bounds.

The techniques employed by the latter are numerous and often ingenious, and here is a brief, non-exhaustive list[10] :

- *Smurfing is one of* the most widely used methods in the industry and involves dividing a total transaction of a certain amount into several transactions divided between several people. Each of these people can then deposit these various sums in bank accounts, with the amount of each, after division, below the reporting threshold, thus avoiding attracting suspicion.

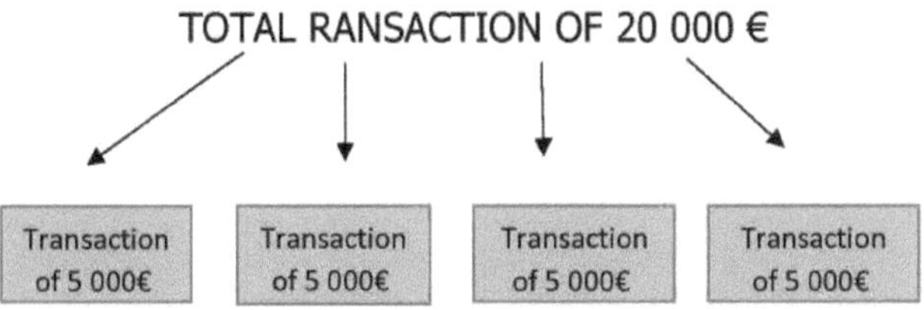

This technique requires good logistics between the participants in the operation but is not necessarily very costly, which justifies its widespread success.

- Bank complicity can also contribute to certain techniques, one of the best

---

[10] **The fight against money laundering,** *Pierre Kopp* in "Analyse économique comparée de la lutte antiblanchiment : droit continental versus Common-Law" 2006

known of which is **self-lending, whereby** money launderers are assisted in their operations by one or more bank employees with a view to facilitating the laundering process.

Using this technique, certain fictitious loans can be granted by complicit banks, even though in reality the sum loaned corresponds to a deposit of an equivalent amount previously made by the money launderer in a bank account. The bank will then return this sum to the money launderer in the form of a fictitious loan agreement, with supporting documents, in order to give a legitimate appearance to the capital transferred. In return, a repayment schedule will be set up, adding to the legitimacy of the operation and providing the money launderer with another means of transferring illegal funds in complete security.

Of course, such practices are becoming more and more difficult with the proliferation of national and international provisions and texts instituting greater supervision and control over the activities of credit institutions.

- **Setting up offshore companies or trusts**[11] in countries with lax anti-money laundering regulations and/or strong banking secrecy. In this way, the money can pass through these legal entities without their composition being revealed.
- Another technique used by criminal organisations is **the organisation of bogus lawsuits**. The principle is that the money launderer organises a bogus lawsuit through one of his companies against another accomplice on the basis of a fictitious loss (false unpaid invoices, for example) which will be settled in private arbitration, at the end of which the first company will have to pay damages to the second. The sum thus paid at the end of the arbitration will serve as the legal basis for an initially illegal financial transaction.

Finally, the third and last phase of the money laundering process, **known as the** *Integration Stage*, simply aims to spend or reinvest the laundered funds in the formal economy, in the same way as any other individual.

According to numerous FATF reports, these investments have three main purposes[12] :

- The acquisition of goods for the personal enrichment of money launderers, such as luxury goods, cars, residences, etc.

---

[11] A trust is a legal entity made up of individuals or companies contributing assets or cash to the trust, which is responsible for managing these assets in accordance with the instructions given to it by the creators of the trust. Trusts are often used to facilitate inheritance or to temporarily separate assets from a company or individual, making it easier to conceal the traceability of funds for money laundering purposes.

[12] **La technique et les pratiques du blanchiment,** Michel Koutouzis, Jean-François Thony, **"Le blanchiment",** 2005, Presses Universitaires de France

- The development and improvement of criminal activities by reinvesting the capital obtained in various money laundering tools, in particular certain shell companies known in the jargon as "washing machines". The latter are in fact commercial activities that process a large quantity of their transactions in cash, such as casinos and restaurants, thus constituting an effective instrument for reinjecting dirty money into the legal economic circuit[13] .
- Legal reinvestment in various financial, property or stock market operations, with a view to generating new sources of income, this time legal, thus enabling a kind of diversification of the activities of criminal organisations. These investments are made with a view to attracting attention, particularly in terms of the scale of the operations, and aim to involve the most important personalities who, through their participation and influence, will guarantee the success of the operation.

  The legitimacy that this confers ultimately acts as a bulwark against any controls for the benefit of money launderers. This practice is now widespread in both emerging and developed countries, although it is slightly less apparent in the latter. At the end of the day, we are no longer simply witnessing the laundering of the criminal's profits, but the laundering of the criminal himself. This third investment purpose is also widely used by terrorist organisations to finance public facilities, hospitals and schools in devastated regions in order to establish their presence and legitimacy among the population.

As this stage completes the money laundering process, there is a virtual novation between the legal and the illegal, between the vulnerable and the untouchable, which, through regular repetition, gradually establishes a system that is virtually unchallengeable.

One of the most striking cases to illustrate this analysis of the stages of money laundering is that of the *"Pizza Connection"*. This process, set up in the late 1970s, enabled the distribution and laundering of a vast heroin trade in the North and Midwest of the United States until 1984, when it was dismantled. This was organised through a chain of "washing machine" businesses, such as restaurants, fishmongers and pizzerias, enabling heroin to be moved from Turkey, the stronghold of Turkish drug baron Müsullulu, to the northern United States. According to historians[14] , a system of payment in stages was put in place whereby drugs were paid for each time they passed through a "relay". In this way, the Cosa Nostra based in America indirectly followed the progress of the merchandise and paid for it as it went along.

---

[13] Cf. above P. 6: **placement phase**
[14] **The Money Launderers: Lessons from the Drug Wars,** *Robert E. Powis*

If we compare this system with the various layers of the money laundering process described above, we can see that this set-up fulfils both the investment phase and the stacking phase. The sums remunerating the "wholesalers" based in Turkey were issued in the form of false supply invoices by the "washing machine" businesses, thus completing the investment stage by injecting the money into the formal economy. Lastly, the "relay" payment route contributed to the piling-up stage by multiplying the transactions, thereby removing the traceability of the funds from the source, i.e. the Turkish trafficker.

§3 The need for an international fight against money laundering

Such an arrangement is not an isolated one in the history of money laundering, since many others were set up during the 20th century, but the American administration (most of the operations took place on American soil) was content to combat these crimes on the basis of federal laws.

It was not until the Colombian cartels set up a cross-border distribution and money laundering network between Colombia and Florida in the 80s, under the aegis of Pablo Escobar, that the American government had to resolve to put in place an anti-money laundering system commensurate with the gigantic economic power that these criminal organisations had acquired through their activities. In fact, given the scale of their activities in the twentieth century, this power could ultimately lead to the establishment of a real counter-power that could have had an unprecedented impact on every stratum of society: corruption of political leaders, destabilisation of banking systems and financial markets through the loss of investor confidence, imbalance in free competition between private players through racketeering and intimidation - no one would have been spared.

In addition to these economic reasons, the United States in the first instance, as well as other countries greatly affected by drug trafficking, saw the fight against money laundering as an effective means of hitting the criminal organisations involved in such activities. The underlying objective was to deprive these mafia networks of the income from their illicit activities by preventing them from giving them a licit appearance, and thus strike an indirect blow at the heart of their activity.

The international community's response to this growing underground economy was to set up the FATF, the first intergovernmental organisation responsible for combating money laundering and the first body to lay the foundations, through its numerous investigations and recommendations, for genuine international cooperation against these many clandestine networks.

Despite such fervour on the part of governments in the fight against money laundering, the task remained a major one, even though a number of "success stories" could be linked to the establishment of such intergovernmental cooperation. Among these, the BCCI collapse remains a benchmark case for *rogue banking*[15] , which was described in 1988 by CIA deputy director Robert Gates as the "*Bank of Crooks and Criminal International*".

Following Operation *C-Chase*[16] , during which a US customs agent, Robert Mazur, infiltrated a BCCI branch in Florida with a view to exposing its links with South American cocaine and heroin trafficking networks, the regulatory authorities in the various countries where the bank was based gradually requested that it cease trading. Investigations eventually revealed that the BCCI was actively providing services and financial support to international drug trafficking networks, terrorists and even dictators, while protecting itself from possible control by the authorities through major political support[17] . Today, the BCCI bankruptcy is one of the most important cases of the use of the financial system for criminal purposes.

As similar cases of varying magnitude came to light, state and international institutions began to recognise the ability of criminal organisations to use the banking and financial system to commit offences, and the importance of combating money laundering and, more recently, the financing of terrorism.

The need for effective global cooperation to achieve these objectives was therefore obvious.

However, with financial crime linked to money laundering evolving rapidly, the authorities very quickly realised that they needed to be constantly reactive, which in practice presents real difficulties. Today, the measures introduced often prove to be out of step with the various techniques put in place by these "shadow networks" and, moreover, the introduction of these measures sometimes finds itself in conflict with certain national laws, thus further hampering the possibility of an effective fight against money laundering.

These findings raise a number of questions, two of which will be the focus of our attention and will serve as a guideline throughout our study: ***who are the main players and what resources have been put in place to combat money laundering? What difficulties do they face in carrying out their mission?***

Indeed, such issues appear to be legitimate, as the organised and coordinated implementation of such a fight has required a great deal of upstream analysis and

---

[15] Anglo-Saxon expression used to designate a criminal bank, literally "swindler's bank".

[16] ***"Infiltrator",*** directed in 2016 by Brad Furman, is the film adaptation of Operation C- CHASE.

[17] BCCI enjoyed the support of figures such as Andrew Young, former mayor of Atlanta and US ambassador to the UN, and Jimmy Carter, 39ème President of the United States of America. However, the latter later claimed to have had no knowledge of the illicit activities carried out by the bank.

preparation through the establishment of institutions and bodies responsible for combating money laundering **(I)**, followed by effective application within each State's legal and economic system, in all sectors likely to be in direct or indirect contact with such clandestine networks **(II)**.

CHAPTER 1

<u>Anti-money laundering institutions and bodies, key players in the fight against underground networks.</u>

Before it was organised and coordinated as it is today, the fight against money laundering was not recognised at international level, and in some countries was not recognised at all. For example, the United States already recognised the act of money laundering as a federal offence, through various texts that gradually extended its scope[18] , while other countries had only the most cursory legislation, which made all those specialised in black finance very happy.

Following numerous multilateral discussions and negotiations, it was not until the establishment of the FATF at the 15ème G7 Summit (known as the Ark Summit) in Paris in 1989 that a real commitment to the fight against money laundering was launched at international level.

The creation of such an institution with an international scope set off a veritable dynamic which gradually led to the creation of a multitude of bodies aimed at countering the proliferation of money laundering activities. Initially set up at international level, these institutions mobilised their efforts within the framework of investigations leading to the establishment of non-binding standards for States **(A)**, within which dedicated bodies were established to combat money laundering on a national scale **(B)**.

A) <u>Global anti-money laundering organisations</u>

As is customary in international law, various types of organisation coexist which, although they all have a global reach, are primarily intended to act at international (Section I) or regional (Section II) level.

The same applies to those working to combat money laundering.

Section I   International organisations

Following the conclusion of international conventions between States with a view to strengthening their cooperation, various organisations were set up to specifically combat money laundering, one of the major bodies being the FATF (§1). These organisations very often work in full collaboration with other international bodies which contribute to the fight against money laundering in a non-specific manner, in parallel with other activities (§2).

---

[18] The US Congress has progressively strengthened its anti-money laundering legislation through three main pieces of legislation: The Bank Secrecy Act (1970), The Money Laundering Control Act (1986) and Title III of The USA Patriot Act (passed in 2001 following the September 11 attacks).

§1 The FATF: the most advanced international instrument specialising in the fight against money laundering

Faced with the growing threat posed by money laundering to the financial world and the banking system, and fearing that such abuses could lead to a systemic risk, the members of the G7 met at the Arche Summit in Paris in 1989 to set up an institution to identify, contain and combat the danger posed by these clandestine networks. The result was the Financial Action *Task Force (TAFT), which* initially comprised the G7 countries[19] , the European Commission (then chaired by Jacques Delors) and 8 other countries[20] .

The Task Force's mission was clear: it was to be an independent international body responsible for "examining money laundering techniques and trends, considering existing national and international action and presenting the measures needed to combat money laundering"[21] .

Originally, the FATF was not intended to have a clear structure or an unlimited lifespan, but was required to review its mission every 5 years. Its decision-making body, made up of representatives of the member states, meets three times a year and takes its decisions on the basis of consensus.

Less than a year after its creation, the FATF's studies and investigations had already borne fruit, as it published its 1[er] report in April 1990, consisting of the "*Forty Recommendations of the FATF*" aimed at establishing an action plan to achieve its objective. With these recommendations, the Action Group sought to establish a common basis for international cooperation with a view to harmonising national legislation. Despite the many revisions that have been made[22] , these recommendations are still the international benchmark in the fight against money laundering.

Over the years, the Action Group has become so important on the international scene that no fewer than twenty States and a new regional organisation[23] have joined its ranks, bringing the FATF to its current 37 members. In addition to its permanent members, the Action Group has three States and around twenty international

---

[19] At the time, the G7 comprised France, the United States, Germany, the United Kingdom, Japan, Italy and Canada.

[20] The 8 non-G7 countries that are original members are : Belgium, Austria, Australia, Luxembourg, the Netherlands, Spain, Sweden and Switzerland.

[21] **History of the FATF,** *FATF press release*

[22] The FATF's *"40 Recommendations" were* revised several times in 1996, 2001 and 2003. The most recent revision, in February 2012, merged the "*40 Recommendations*" with the "*9 Special Recommendations*" on the financing of terrorism and the proliferation of weapons of mass destruction, the 2001 revision having extended the FATF's mandate to include the fight against the financing of terrorism.

[23] The 16 original members have been joined by Argentina, Brazil, China, the Republic of Korea, Denmark, Russia, Finland, Greece, Hong Kong, Iceland, India, Ireland, Malaysia, Mexico, New Zealand, Norway, Portugal, Singapore, South Africa, Turkey and a regional organisation, the Gulf Cooperation Council.

organisations with observer status, including Israel, Indonesia, Saudi Arabia, the IMF, the World Bank, Interpol, Europol, etc.

As set out in its original statute, the FATF's task is to draw up non-binding standards to enable the creation of effective legislative, regulatory and operational provisions in the various countries with a view to preserving the integrity of the international financial system in the face of the dangers of money laundering (and, more recently, the financing of terrorism). The Action Group has therefore gradually been given a degree of non-binding regulatory power. Moreover, although its recommendations are non-binding, they often take the form of obligations towards States, with the FATF regularly compiling a list of non-cooperative States, thus contributing to this "implicit regulatory power".

Indeed, with a view to achieving this objective, and indirectly with a view to the progressive harmonisation of national provisions on money laundering, the Action Group monitors the work carried out by States, starting with its own members, in implementing its recommendations. It is on the basis of this ongoing monitoring that the FATF draws up a list of high-risk and/or non-cooperative jurisdictions, which is communicated in one of the two documents it publishes annually.

These documents, entitled respectively *"The FATF Public Statement"* and *"Improving Global AML/CFT Compliance[24] : An Ongoing Process"*, are revised and published at each plenary meeting of the Action Group (3 times a year) and draw up a list of countries with *"strategic AML/CFT deficiencies"*[25] . In the first document, the organisation presents the countries concerned that have not made or do not wish to make efforts to improve their AML/CFT legislation and against which the Member States and other States must apply countermeasures to protect the integrity of their financial system[26]. The second identifies States with similar strategic deficiencies that wish to remedy them by means of an action plan drawn up in collaboration with the FATF.

To identify such deficiencies, the Financial Action Task Force uses techniques other than traditional mutual evaluation programmes. Between 2000 and 2006, the organisation launched *the PTNC Procedure*[27] , during which it identified 23 countries with significant AML/CFT risks. In the end, the procedure achieved its objective with flying colours, as all of these countries were removed from the NCCT list at the end of

---

[24] AML/CFT: Acronym for "fight against money laundering/terrorist financing".

[25] **High-risk and non-cooperative jurisdictions,** *FATF Communiqué*

[26] It is through these calls that the FATF has enjoined its member states and invited other countries to apply effective counter-measures against Iran and the Democratic People's Republic of Korea, from February 2009 and February 2011 to the present day.

[27] PTNC: Acronym for "Non-Cooperative Countries and Territories".

the procedure.

Similarly, in 2007 the FATF set up the International Cooperation Review Group (ICRG) to identify high-risk countries and territories with a view to addressing their AML/CFT problems. This committee of experts saw its prerogatives strengthened in 2009 following a call from the G20 Heads of State and Government for the FATF to relaunch the process of assessing countries' compliance with international AML/CFT standards. As part of its powers, the GECI draws up a report on the basis of which the FATF will decide to put in place measures to counter the deficiencies of the country concerned, either through countermeasures or by establishing an action plan in collaboration with the country concerned.

The various monitoring mechanisms set up by the FATF have led to a clear improvement in some countries' anti-money laundering measures, as was the case for Greece in June 2011 and Ukraine in October 2011, among other examples. Despite this, a number of problems remain, casting a shadow over the unblemished record of the FATF's work in recent years.

The Financial Action Task Force was set up by the G8 member states at the Ark Summit in response to concerns in industrialised countries that the banking and financial system was being used fraudulently by criminal organisations. It is clear from the *FATF's 40 Recommendations*, which form the basic framework for its action, that the use of the financial system by criminal or mafia organisations will be the FATF's main target.

The intention of the FATF's founding States was thus to follow on from *the 1988 Vienna Convention*[28] , which at the time was already intended to combat the organised crime of drug traffickers and to introduce new incriminating measures relating in particular to the laundering of money linked to the resale of drugs. This intention was in no way disguised, as the FATF made this convention its legal basis.

Similarly, in 1990, *the Council of Europe Convention on money laundering*[29] reiterated the objective of combating "serious" crime by fighting money laundering. These factors clearly demonstrate the desire at the time to combat criminal organisations by combating money laundering, which was not only a source of income for these organisations but also their funding. This was to be the real purpose of the FATF, to combat money laundering directly in order to contribute indirectly to the fight against criminal organisations.

---

[28] *The 1988 Convention against Illicit Traffic in Narcotic Drugs and Psychotropic Substances* (also known as the 1988 Vienna Convention) is a United Nations convention designed to strengthen the provisions against drug trafficking previously put in place by the 1961 and 1971 UN conventions.

[29] *The Strasbourg Convention on Laundering, Search, Seizure and Confiscation of the Proceeds from Crime of 8 November 1990*, ratified within the framework of the Council of Europe.

In the end, the Financial Action Task Force failed in its mission, since the anti-money laundering mechanism established through its *40 recommendations did* not succeed in hitting its initial target, criminal organisations, which quickly found new techniques to develop their activities. However, it did manage to put in place an effective process for combating economic and financial crime, which was not initially envisaged by the "creators" of the FATF, by considerably locking down the financial system. Under the guise of fighting criminal organisations, the introduction of new standards designed to establish greater transparency within the banking and financial sector was more easily accepted by the business world, despite the real upheaval that these standards could create in the sector.

The second stumbling block for the FATF, despite the scope of its work, concerns the legal problems raised by its recommendations.

By way of comparison, the 1988 Vienna Convention, which was an essential source of inspiration for the creation of the FATF, had the advantage of introducing a number of innovations compared with the other conventions dealing with the fight against drugs. These included the possibility of confiscating the proceeds of narcotics trafficking (mainly income) or property the value of which corresponds to these proceeds[30] as well as a reversal of the burden of proof regarding the lawful origin of these presumed illicit proceeds. But the real contribution of the Vienna Convention was its drafting, which used clear and precise legal language, thereby enabling relatively uniform national transposition within the States parties.

The *40 Recommendations,* for their part, set out a series of measures and standards that were not legal but ethical in nature, most of them constituting guidelines for good professional practice, mainly with regard to credit and financial institutions. The main stumbling block arising from such a choice was that not only was it impossible to achieve quasi-uniform harmonisation between States, but also that transposition into criminal law appeared tricky, given the broad and imprecise nature of the concepts used.[31] It was in this respect that the FATF won its battle against economic and financial crime, but lost the battle against criminal organisations.

Of course, in addition to these unresolved issues, the FATF's work today remains considerable and will have made a major contribution to the fight against money laundering and, more recently, the financing of terrorism. But such progress has only been possible thanks to the cooperation that the FATF has received from other

---

[30] The other conventions only provided for the possibility of confiscating narcotics, substances and equipment used to produce narcotics.

[31] This was the case in France, which adopted the law of 12 July 1990 providing for the introduction of disciplinary sanctions only against recalcitrant banking and financial establishments by means of an administrative procedure to the detriment of criminal transposition.

international organisations involved in the fight against money laundering.

§2 <u>International support organisations in the fight against money laundering</u>

As the fight against money laundering is primarily organised through enhanced global cooperation, many international organisations are involved in it alongside their other functions. By virtue of their role, these organisations are attached to the FATF as observers, a status which puts them in the front line when decisions are taken by the Action Group.

The list of observer organisations is long and fairly heterogeneous, coming from the banking sector, the United Nations and the financial world. However, what they all have in common is that they are intergovernmental organisations. The FATF establishes a certain number of criteria that must be met before an international organisation can acquire observer status with the Action Group. These include the condition of being an intergovernmental organisation, which de facto excludes any non-governmental organisation (NGO) wishing to participate in FATF missions. This may be justified by the Action Group's great caution with regard to NGOs, particularly in the context of the fight against the financing of terrorism[32] .

Prudence is one of the key points on which the criteria are based, with the FATF placing particular emphasis on the clarity of the motivations and the role that applicant international organisations wish to assume. Similarly, the Action Group expects effective cooperation with these organisations through the establishment of reciprocity, particularly in the exchange of information, but also through the expansion and strengthening of its geographical reach.

Once observer status has been obtained, the international organisations are assigned a role, corresponding to their respective areas of expertise and activity, which will facilitate or contribute to the success of the FATF's various missions.

For example, Interpol[33] participates as an observer and is one of the key elements of the FATF network. Interpol is a key ally within the Action Group, particularly since the establishment of the *Millennium Project to* share information via its huge database and its global police communications system known as *I-24/7, giving* investigators around the world direct access to a wealth of information on money laundering. Interpol also has an Anti-Money Laundering Unit, whose officers are located around the world and act as contact points for anyone involved in the fight against money

---

[32] Cf. *IX Special Recommendations of the FATF*

[33] Based in Lyon, Interpol is the world's largest international police organisation. It provides a permanent link between the police forces of 190 countries with a view to providing them with technical and operational support in the fight against crime, particularly through the discovery of links between various investigations taking place in different countries.

laundering. This unit also aims to establish optimum co-operation between the Financial Intelligence Units[34] (FIUs), particularly in the sharing of information, but also with the other international organisations involved.

Finally, as the fight against the financing of terrorism has become a major challenge for the FATF, it can count on Interpol's anti-terrorism task force (known as the Fusion Task Force), which is responsible for gathering information, identifying members and the money transfer techniques most commonly used by terrorist organisations.

In addition to the significant logistical support provided by international organisations such as Interpol, the FATF also benefits from the recognised expertise of global banking and financial institutions such as the IMF[35].

The IMF makes a major contribution to the fight against money laundering, with two of its departments specifically responsible for implementing projects in this area: the Financial Systems Department and the Legal Department. What's more, because of its global reach and the fact that its membership includes almost every country in the world, the International Monetary Fund represents *"a natural forum for sharing information, developing common approaches and promoting desirable policies and standards"*[36].

The IMF has become more involved in the fight against money laundering alongside the FATF, recognising the *40 Recommendations and* the *Special IXs* as a standard on the basis of which it has undertaken to produce its *Reports on the Observance of Standards and Codes* (ROSCs)[37]. As part of these reports, the IMF assesses the measures applied in the fight against money laundering and terrorist financing in the various countries, thereby making a major contribution to the achievement of the FATF's objectives.

Numerous international bodies have rallied to the FATF's cause by becoming more involved in the fight against money laundering. This has been particularly the case for the United Nations, no fewer than six of whose entities have joined the Action Group as observers. Among these, the United Nations Office on Drugs and Crime (UNODC)[38]

---

[34] The Financial Intelligence Units are the specialised anti-money laundering bodies established in each country. TRACFIN is the French FIU.

[35] Created on 22 July 1944 under the **Bretton Woods Agreement**, the International Monetary Fund is an organisation dedicated to the maintenance of global financial stability, international monetary cooperation and the development of sustainable economic growth, with the ultimate aim of increasing employment, raising the standard of living of the middle classes and reducing poverty.

[36] Cf. **International Monetary Fund**, *FATF Communiqué*

[37] The ROSC, which stands for *Report on the Observance of Standards and Codes*, was drawn up in collaboration with the IMF and the World Bank following the recent international financial crises, and aims to establish a set of standards and codes of good practice in economic and financial management that are universal in scope. The correct application of these standards is periodically reassessed in reports.

[38] The *United Nations Office on Drugs and* Crime (UNODC) is a United Nations body founded in 1997, following the merger of the *United Nations International Drug Control Programme* (UNDCP) and the *United Nations Centre for*

plays a key role in the FATF's fight against clandestine networks, notably through its Organised Crime and Money Laundering Unit. The undeniable advantage of the UN's participation in the Action Group's mission is the possibility of recourse to the various international instruments put in place by the United Nations[39] , thereby considerably broadening the means of action available to the FATF.

It is clear that the concerted action of these various international organisations has made a major contribution to the progress made in recent years in the fight against money laundering, despite some stumbling blocks. Moreover, such a fight cannot always be waged on a global scale, as is the case with these organisations, and requires the introduction of measures tailored to the specific circumstances of each country in the world. This is where regional organisations come into their own.

Section II   Regional organisations

As the fight against money laundering is organised at different levels, global organisations with a regional scope are essential for optimum application of the standards established at international level (§2). Among these, the European Union[40] plays a crucial role due to the authority it has over its Member States (§1).

§1 The European Union's involvement in the fight against money laundering

A large proportion of organised crime and financial delinquency is to be found in Europe[41] and the Old Continent therefore has a strategic role to play in the fight against money laundering. The former European Community was aware of this and, with the directive of 10 June 1991[42] , attempted to introduce the first semblance of measures against money laundering. However, it was not until the Geneva Appeal of 1er October 1996[43] , voiced by 7 leading judges, that the European States became truly aware of the problem.

Numerous texts were subsequently adopted within the framework of the European

---

International Crime Prevention (UNCICP), to assist UN member states in their fight against crime, drug trafficking and terrorism.

[39] Mainly *the 1988 Vienna Convention against Illicit Traffic in Narcotic Drugs and Psychotropic Substances* and the *2000 Palermo Convention against Transnational Organised Crime.*

[40] Although the European Union is a sui generis political and economic entity, we will consider it to be a regional organisation in the course of this study because its scope is restricted to its Member States.

[41] Particularly through the Italian Mafia families and the criminal organisations of Eastern Europe.

[42] **The Council Directive of 10 June 1991 on the prevention of the use of the financial system for the purpose of money laundering** incorporated many elements of the 1988 Vienna Convention and established a number of obligations for credit and financial institutions. This was **the I**ère **European anti-money laundering directive**.

[43] **The Geneva Call of 1er October 1996 was a** public request by 7 European anti-corruption magistrates for the establishment of a common judicial area within Europe to combat the laundering of tax fraud and the proceeds of criminal activities, which particularly affected Europe at the end of the 20th century.

Union, instituting various instruments with the aim of establishing an ever stronger fight against money laundering and increasingly necessary judicial cooperation between Member States. Some progress was made, notably with the first discussions on *Eurojust*[44] during the Tampere European Council summit in 1999[45] , then with the signing of the Convention on Mutual Assistance in Criminal Matters between the Member States of 29 May 2000[46] and its anti-money laundering protocol of 16 October 2001, as well as with the agreement reached on the European arrest warrant during the Laeken European Council of 14 December 2001.

The various provisions thus established by the European Union have an advantage over other texts adopted by international organisations in the fight against money laundering in that they do not limit the measures instituted solely to drug trafficking[47] . However, these provisions only apply to EU Member States.

These measures were important steps forward in the fight against money laundering, although they went relatively unnoticed[48] . However, the 2001 Money Laundering Protocol, for example, contained a number of interesting provisions, obliging Member States to establish more effective judicial cooperation in the financial and banking sector.

Article 1[er] of the Directive set out an obligation on Member States to achieve results by applying measures at national level to determine whether a natural or legal person held or controlled one or more bank accounts in their territory. With this measure, the European Union sought to put an end to the shortcomings still experienced by too many Member States in terms of bank information, while leaving them the choice of the method applied.

In this way, the EU aimed to introduce a degree of harmonisation in the investigative resources of the Member States, while at the same time raising the issue of banking secrecy, which credit and financial institutions all too often used, hampering all efforts to combat money laundering. This idea was also taken up in Article 7 of the Protocol, which stipulated that banking secrecy could not constitute a legitimate ground for rejecting a request for mutual assistance from a Member State.

---

[44] *Eurojust, or the European Union's Judicial Cooperation Unit*, is an EU body responsible for promoting judicial cooperation between Member States through the adoption of structural measures. Initially discussed at **the Tampere Summit in 1999**, it was finally adopted by a Council decision on 28 February 2002.

[45] **The European Council Summit of 15 and 16 October 1999 in Tampere** was organised with a view to formalising effective European judicial cooperation, following on from the **1997 Treaty of Amsterdam.**

[46] This convention included a set of provisions relating to the procedure for requesting mutual assistance between Member States.

[47] **The 1990 Council of Europe Convention in Strasbourg did** not limit the scope of application to drug trafficking in the same way as the EU.

[48] **The anti-money laundering protocol of 16 October 2001 was** not mentioned in the final declaration of the conference of European Union parliaments against money laundering of 8 February 2002.

The conclusion of the agreement on the introduction of a European Arrest Warrant in 2001 also enabled significant progress to be made by putting an end to extradition procedures between Member States within the scope of this text, thus providing an additional tool in the fight against money laundering networks.

Of course, these measures were originally introduced with a view to mutual legal assistance between Member States, but they may have been the first steps on a long and difficult journey.

Following on from this work, the European Union supplemented the 1991 directive with a new directive dated 4 December 2001[49] significantly strengthening the fight against money laundering. Under the old 1991 directive, banking and financial institutions were required to obtain information on their customers, based on the KYC concept[50] , to keep all documents relating to them and to introduce internal anti-money laundering measures. In addition, the directive also required credit and financial institutions to lift their banking secrecy in the event of a suspicion of money laundering concerning one of their customers.

Although this directive has been widely transposed within the European Union, it quickly became a "victim of its own success", as such a tight lockdown of the banking and financial sector led criminal organisations to shift their money laundering proceeds to other professions.

It was for this reason that in July 1999, at the request of the European Parliament, the Commission tabled a proposal to extend the 1991 directive, which led to the adoption of the new directive on 4 December 2001.

With this directive, the European Union significantly strengthened its anti-money laundering measures by broadening the scope of its provisions. As a result, it was considered that the definition of money laundering was no longer limited to the proceeds of drug trafficking, but could be extended to all trafficking and organised crime networks, and that KYC and suspicious transaction reporting obligations should be extended to all professions considered likely to be in contact with money laundering networks, such as notaries, lawyers, legal advisers and auctioneers.

The first two European anti-money laundering directives were finally repealed by another directive of 26 October 2005[51] which incorporated all their content but extended their scope to include the fight against terrorist financing. Finally, the EU subsequently introduced new anti-money laundering provisions in the *Regulation of*

---

[49] This directive of 4 December 2001 was the IIème European anti-money laundering directive.

[50] KYC, which stands for 'Know Your Customer', is an international behavioural standard that requires banking and financial institutions to exercise due diligence in relation to their customers.

[51] This directive constitutes the IIIème European anti-money laundering directive.

15 November 2006 on information on the payer accompanying transfers of funds[52] , although the latter is not specific to the fight against money laundering.

The European Union's work on money laundering then turned to the area of shell companies and trusts, with the aim of setting up a list in each Member State containing the names and details of the beneficial owners of legal entities.

The EU's sudden interest in this particular type of company followed the *"Luxleaks"* financial scandal at the end of 2014, in which the International Consortium of Investigative Journalists revealed the existence of hundreds of tax agreements between Luxembourg and certain companies involving the introduction of *tax rulings[53]* more than advantageous to the latter.

But introducing such measures was tricky.

An initial vote was taken by MEPs adopting the legislative resolution on the anti-money laundering directive, which was then intended to become the fourth European directive. The challenge for the Parliament was to resist the various pressures from the Council, as the Member States were reluctant to adopt such a list. A compromise was reached on 18 December 2014[54] providing that only trusts generating taxable income would be included on the list and that the list would not be public in all Member States, being accessible to journalists only on presentation of a "legitimate reason".

The text was finally passed by Parliament on 20 May 2015, becoming **the IV**[ème] **European anti-money laundering directive**. As part of its ongoing drive to comply with international standards, the EU has included a number of new features in the text to ensure that its provisions are compatible with the FATF's *"40 Recommendations"*.

Firstly, the scope of the directive has been strengthened once again by including gambling service providers and traders in goods for cash transactions of €10,000 or more. Similarly, the concept of Politically Exposed Persons (PEPs)[55] has been extended to nationals and senior executives of international organisations.

With regard to the beneficial owners of legal persons, important measures were also introduced to ensure that an up-to-date register was kept containing all relevant information concerning them. To this end, the Member States were obliged to introduce national provisions for identifying these beneficiaries. Contrary to the initial

---

[52] The main purpose of this regulation was to transpose into EU legislation the FATF's *Special Recommendation VII* on wire transfers, which requires financial institutions to include specific information on the originator when transferring funds.

[53] *Tax rulings* are formal statements made by the tax authorities in response to a query from a taxpayer. These tax rulings are enforceable against the tax authorities, even if they are contrary to the law.

[54] **La directive anti-blanchiment vidée de son ambition de transparence,** 18 December 2014, *EurActiv*

[55] PPE, Cf. below P.56

intention, this list was not intended to be accessible to the public, although access to the register could be granted to other taxable persons as part of their duty of due diligence, as well as to any interested person with a legitimate reason. In addition, the EU gave Member States the option of introducing public access to the register.

Finally, through various provisions, the Directive strengthened the European anti-money laundering system through greater cooperation between national FIUs and by increasing the penalties applicable in the various Member States.

Finally, it should be noted that, in parallel with the introduction of the IVème Directive, on 20 May 2015 the European Parliament also adopted the *Regulation on information accompanying transfers of funds*, repealing the previous text of November 2006 and including in particular the new provisions relating to beneficial owners.

As the new directive had only just been introduced, the European Union set a deadline of 26 June 2017 for Member States to transpose it into national law. However, a number of events prompted MEPs to revise their plans sooner than expected.

Following the terrorist attacks that hit Europe between 2015 and 2016 and the *Panama Papers* scandal in April 2016, the European Commission presented a new proposal on 5 July 2016 aimed at further strengthening the provisions for combating money laundering and terrorist financing.

Following discussions, the **Vème European Anti-Money Laundering Directive** was finally adopted on 30 May 2018, further increasing its scope and once again strengthening the powers of FIUs. One of its main contributions was the introduction of provisions on the use of virtual currencies in the fight against terrorist financing. Finally, in the wake of the *Panama Papers*, measures were also introduced to ensure greater vigilance over transactions involving countries considered to be at risk and their nationals.

All the work carried out by the European Union in the fight against money laundering shows that the standards established by the FATF in its *40 Recommendations* have had a major influence. Indeed, many of the key provisions of the EU directives on money laundering are linked to the 40 recommendations: the introduction of mutual legal assistance is provided for in recommendations 36 to 40, the duty of due diligence is mentioned in recommendation 10ème , etc...

It is also interesting to note that the European Commission is one of the 36 members sitting on the FATF's plenary assemblies, which is then responsible within the European Union, among other functions, for submitting proposals for directives to the Council and Parliament. This facilitates the transposition of these recommendations within the EU.

However, it should be noted that the European Union has not yet fully incorporated into its directives the measures to combat the proliferation of weapons of mass destruction, as recommended by the FATF in its 7ème recommendation.

In the end, it appears that the European Union is contributing to a degree of global harmonisation of anti-money laundering standards by incorporating them into its body of texts and then imposing them on its Member States by way of directives. This is precisely where the participation of regional organisations comes in: the close application of FATF recommendations in specific sectors, as is also done by "*FATF-type*" organisations.

§2 <u>FATF-type organisations: direct collaborators of the Action Group at regional level</u>

In its desire to build an ever more effective global network to combat money laundering and terrorist financing, the Action Group has gradually surrounded itself with "FATF-type" regional bodies responsible for carrying out tasks similar to its own within the geographical area to which they apply.

These organisations are then assigned a certain number of objectives, arising from their status as "associate members" of the FATF, aimed at contributing to the fulfilment of the Task Force's missions. These include approving and recognising the FATF's recommendations and various standards, promoting the effective application of these standards within their member states, organising mutual evaluation reviews using the methodology recommended by the Action Group and participating in the development of the FATF's standards and other policies to combat money laundering[56] . Associate membership is not granted automatically, of course, and all applications are examined by the Plenary Assembly, which will then decide whether to involve the applicant organisations in the work of the FATF.

There are currently 9 FATF-style regional organisations that have acquired the rank of associate member and between them they share almost the entire world territory, thereby significantly increasing the scope of application of the FATF's recommendations and standards.

At European level, the Action Group can rely on MONEYVAL[57] , a group of experts set up in 1997 by the Committee of Ministers of the Council of Europe, whose role is to support the organisation's member states in implementing effective measures against money laundering and the financing of terrorism. Where appropriate,

---

[56] These responsibilities and objectives are redefined every 8 years, with the current mandate running from 2012 to 2020.

[57] MONEYVAL, also known as the *Committee of Experts on the Evaluation of Anti-Money Laundering Measures and the Financing of Terrorism (formerly PC-R-EV), has been an associate member of the FATF since 2006.*

MONEYVAL can also make recommendations to member states experiencing difficulties in effectively combating money laundering.

In addition to this support role, MONEYVAL also ensures compliance with internationally recognised standards[58] in the field through a monitoring mechanism analysing the measures put in place in the legislation of each Member State. This monitoring, which is also carried out by the FATF, is very useful within the MONEYVAL framework for Member States that are not members of the Action Group. Finally, the organisation also carries out typological and analytical studies on the methods, trends and techniques used by criminal organisations to launder money.

MONEYVAL is just one example, as the FATF has surrounded itself with numerous regional organisations in its aim to progressively harmonise the legislation and instruments put in place by States to combat money laundering. We could also mention the GAFIC[59] whose area of action covers all the States and territories of the Caribbean basin, which is particularly renowned for its high concentration of tax havens, or even the GIABA[60] whose scope of application extends to all the member States of the Economic Community of West Africa.

Through these regional organisations, the FATF has been able to strike a major blow by gradually acquiring crucial partners enabling it to extend its field of action to almost all the countries in the world. Not only do these organisations ensure that the FATF's recommendations are applied precisely, adapted to the culture and specific features of the territories concerned, they also extend the scope of these standards to member states that have not joined the FATF. They thus act as intermediaries for the Action Group, spreading its "word" to its own members.

It would appear that the fight against money laundering initiated by the FATF seems to have gradually organised itself to reach a global reach, personifying the final will of "its creators" discussed during the 1989 Ark Summit. However, the battle is far from over and the road to victory is still long. Although the FATF has succeeded in organising its strategy and extending its reach on a global scale, the war against money laundering and criminal organisations can only be waged on the ground by the various States, which will then have to implement the measures devised by the

---

[58] MONEYVAL ensures compliance with the standards set by the FATF **(40 + IX recommendations)** as well as UN texts (the **1988 Vienna Convention and the 2000 Palermo Convention**) and EU directives on the **prevention of the use of the financial system for money laundering and terrorist financing**. Of course, MONEYVAL is also based on **the Council of Europe's Strasbourg Convention on Laundering, Search, Seizure and Confiscation of the Proceeds from Crime of 8 November 1990.**

[59] *GAFIC for Groupe d'Action Financière des Caraïbes* was created following 2 founding meetings in Aruba in May 1990 then in Jamaica in November 1992.

[60] *GIABA stands for Groupe Intergouvernemental d'Action contre le blanchiment d'argent en Afrique de l'Ouest (Intergovernmental Action Group against Money Laundering in West Africa)*, established in 2000 following the Conference of Heads of State and Government of the Economic Community of West African States (ECOWAS).

Financial Action Task Force.

B) <u>French bodies dedicated to combating money laundering</u>

With a view to complying with the recommendations of the FATF and the measures instituted by other international organisations involved in the fight against money laundering, the States have gradually drawn inspiration from these standards in order to create legislation that meets the need for a harmonised defence against the resurgence of these clandestine networks.

France is proud to have been one of[61] 's best pupils, having set up TRACFIN as early as 1990, one year after the Ark Summit. Today, TRACFIN is one of the most highly developed national anti-money laundering bodies in the world (Section I), and also through its administrative authorities responsible for regulating and supervising the banking and financial sector (Section II).

Section I: TRACFIN, France's financial intelligence unit.

Following the 1989 L'Arche Summit, the G7 member states quickly began work on introducing measures to combat money laundering, in particular by setting up national financial intelligence units.

France, for its part, had already passed a law in 1987[62] setting out the first anti-money laundering provisions in the fight against drug trafficking, with the offence of money laundering for drug trafficking being incorporated into the Criminal Code for the first time. However, it now had to meet its international commitments.

It was against this backdrop that TRACFIN[63] was created by *the Act* of 12 July 1990 *on the participation of financial institutions in the fight against money laundering from drug trafficking*[64] as a financial intelligence coordination unit attached to the Directorate General of Customs and Excise. It was not until the decree of 6 December 2006 that TRACFIN became a department with national jurisdiction[65] and then the decree of 7 January 2011 that it was given its own directorate.

TRACFIN, as it exists today, is a body with national competence, under the supervision

---

[61] According to a report by the Cour des Comptes published in 2012, the French anti-money laundering system is one of only three national systems that only has to report on improvements every 2 years.

[62] *The Act of 31 December 1987 on combating drug trafficking* defined for the first time the offence of laundering the proceeds of drug trafficking. It was not until the *Act of 13 May 1996 that* a general offence of laundering the proceeds of all crimes or offences was introduced.

[63] TRACFIN for *Traitement du Renseignement et Action contre les Circuits Financiers clandestins (Information Processing and Action against Illicit Financial Circuits)*

[64] The 1990 Act also led to the creation of the Office Central de Répression de la Grande Délinquance Financière (OCRGDF), a unit of the judicial police responsible for combating money laundering and the financing of terrorism.

[65] The national services (SCN) are administrative services designed to carry out operational missions throughout France, and are governed by two decrees issued in 1997.

of the Ministry of the Economy and Finance, whose objective is to contribute to the development of a healthy economy by combating clandestine financial circuits, money laundering and the financing of terrorism.

Articles L561-23 to L561-31 of the Monetary and Financial Code set out the two main missions entrusted to TRACFIN by the legislator:

- Receiving, analysing, enriching and exploiting information relating to clandestine financial circuits and any transactions that may be linked to money laundering and/or terrorist financing[66] . The same Article L561-23 stipulates that if the department's investigations reveal money laundering operations, it must refer the matter to the public prosecutor on the basis of an information memorandum.
- Exchanging with the supervisory authorities, professional bodies and national representative bodies any information that may be useful in carrying out their respective duties[67] .

It is therefore clear that most of the tasks entrusted to TRACFIN derive from, and depend on, suspicious transaction reports from the persons mentioned in Article L561-2 of the CMF, i.e. banking and financial institutions and, by extension, any person likely to be in contact with money laundering operations. It is only on the basis of these suspicious transaction reports that an administrative investigation can be opened by TRACFIN. In addition, as an administrative FIU ([68]), TRACFIN will never be able to take legal action itself in the event of a money laundering operation and will have to refer the matter to the judicial authorities. It should be noted, however, that in order to protect those subject to the law, the report referred to the Public Prosecutor will not appear in the case file in order to preserve the anonymity of the person making it and that the latter must be informed by TRACFIN of the referral.

To this end, the legislator has given TRACFIN a set of powers which it can use in the course of its work. In particular, TRACFIN has the right to obtain from the professionals concerned by the anti-money laundering measures[69] any documents that may be useful in its investigation (invoices, bank listings, etc.), particularly when the agency is seeking to reconstruct all transactions carried out by an individual or legal entity that has been the subject of an alert. This right of disclosure may be exercised on the basis of documentary evidence, within a time limit set by the body

---

[66] Article L561-23 of the Monetary and Financial Code

[67] Article 561-30 of the Monetary and Financial Code

[68] Administrative FIUs are generally attached to the Ministry of Finance, the central bank or a regulatory body in their country and act as an intermediary between those subject to their control and the judicial or law enforcement authorities. According to the IMF classification, FIUs may be administrative, police, judicial or hybrid.

[69] Article L561-25 of the CMF provides for the right of disclosure to professionals concerned by the anti-money laundering measures.

for the professionals concerned, or on the spot[70] . However, there is an exception for lawyers, as TRACFIN must make its request to the President of the Bar Association in which the lawyer concerned is registered.

In the same vein, TRACFIN will be able to obtain information from any public institution, government agency or local authority likely to hold information that may be of interest to it in the performance of its duties[71] . In addition, the Order of 30 January 2009 now allows TRACFIN to obtain such information from any person entrusted with a public service mission[72] such as URSSAF or trade unions, thereby broadening the scope of this right of communication. Conversely, they may also request information, such as the tax authorities in their fight against fraud. Lastly, under the terms of Articles L561-29 and L561-29-1 of the CMF, this power may be used with other foreign FIUs, which may also ask it to provide them with information in return, if their national legislation allows them to do so.

TRACFIN has a third and final power, which consists of the possibility of objecting to the execution of a financial transaction on the basis of information or declarations, even without first informing the professional responsible for carrying out the transaction[73] . The transaction will thus be neutralised for a period of ten working days from the date of notification, which may be extended by the President of the Paris Tribunal de Grande Instance at the request of TRACFIN or the public prosecutor.

The Banking Separation and Regulation Act of 26 July 2013 also introduced a new procedure for combating money laundering through the Systematic Disclosure of Information (COSI) procedure[74] , which replaces the former Systematic Disclosure of Information (DSO) system. Under the COSI procedure, regulated professionals will be required to report automatically to TRACFIN, using an appropriate IT system, any fund transfers involving cash or electronic money that exceed the threshold of €1,000 or €2,000 per customer over a calendar month. Similarly, all deposits and withdrawals exceeding an aggregate amount of 10,000 euros over a calendar month must also be reported.

Lastly, the Order of 1[er] December 2016 clarified that the COSI procedure applies only to transactions presenting a high risk of money laundering or terrorist financing due to their nature, the legal entities involved or the countries or territories involved. This amendment makes a clearer distinction with the traditional suspicious transaction report provided for in Article L561-15.

---

[70] However, the right of on-site consultation may only be exercised at banking and financial establishments.

[71] This power to communicate with the public is provided for in article L561-27 of the CMF.

[72] This possibility was not initially provided for in the *New Economic Regulations* Act of 2001.

[73] This right of objection is conferred under Article L561-24 of the CMF.

[74] This procedure is defined in article L561-15-1 of the CMF.

This information will not be analysed immediately and cannot in itself be used as a basis for prosecution. It will simply be added to TRACFIN's database with a view to future investigations.

The prerogatives thus conferred on TRACFIN by the legislator give it considerable scope for action to fulfil its mission. These powers are further strengthened by cooperation between the various FIUs worldwide and by TRACFIN's extensive involvement at international level.

This cooperation is made possible in particular through the Egmont Group[75] , within which TRACFIN can benefit from real international support from the other FIUs that are members of the group. Following the drafting of a standard bilateral cooperation agreement, the Egmont Group has set up a secure system for exchanging information via the Internet, giving FIUs access to a near-global database of its 155 members and freeing them from the procedural hurdles of international cooperation requests. As a result, the exchange of information is much more reactive, which in turn improves the effectiveness of the FIU.

Another specific feature of the Egmont Group is the regular organisation of regional workshops aimed at optimising the efficiency of member FIUs through regular training of their agents. During these workshops, officers share their experiences and are presented with concrete cases likely to be encountered in the course of their duties. TRACFIN is therefore particularly involved in the work carried out by the Egmont Group.

Alongside this entity, TRACFIN is also very active in other international bodies combating money laundering. As a member of the French delegation, TRACFIN contributes its experience as an operational body to the FATF in carrying out its typology work and mutual evaluations, as well as to numerous committees within the EU[76] .

The assessment of TRACFIN's work, 25 years after its creation, is therefore fairly positive, as the powers entrusted to the department by the legislator appear to be in line with the anti-money laundering mission with which it is entrusted. However, this positive assessment is qualified by certain shortcomings, particularly with regard to coordination between national anti-money laundering agencies and a lack of material resources allocated to the department to carry out its mission.

---

[75] Created in 1995 in Brussels, the Egmont Group is an informal operational exchange forum for the FIU members of the entity, with the aim of developing genuine international cooperation between them.
TRACFIN was one of the founding members of the Egmont Group

[76] TRACFIN is also a member of the *Financial Intelligence Units Platform* and the *Committee on the Prevention of Money Laundering and Terrorist Financing in the* European Union.

In a report published in February 2012[77] , the Cour des Comptes highlighted a number of problems requiring particular attention in order to improve the effectiveness of the French anti-money laundering system:

- The lack of statistical data on the scale of money laundering, which would enable TRACFIN to gain a better understanding of the phenomenon and anticipate future developments.
- The failure to develop typologies for reporting professions that would enable them to adopt a better "risk-based approach[78] " towards their customers.
- The lack of uniform involvement of the reporting professions in the fight against money laundering, most of which, with the exception of banks and bailiffs, participate only too timidly in the procedure for reporting suspicions. The Cour des Comptes therefore recommends that educational initiatives be organised to make reporting professions aware of the stakes involved in combating money laundering.
- At an organisational level, TRACFIN lacks sufficient and diversified staff, which means that it has to focus its recruitment on more heterogeneous profiles specialising in broader areas.
- Too few court filings due to poor organisation of investigation management and overloading of the service
- Management of the STARTRAC database needs to be optimised to improve its relevance
- The introduction of purely quantitative performance indicators in 2010 prevents them from being properly interpreted by the department. These indicators therefore need to be rethought with a view to providing a qualitative view of performance.
- With regard to the anti-money laundering system as a whole, the Cour des Compt recommends that tax fraud be taken into account more effectively and that both administrative and criminal sanctions be strengthened.

The comments and recommendations made by the Cour des Comptes in this 2012 report were taken on board by the public authorities, which then set about improving the French anti-money laundering system, in particular by releasing additional staff to TRACFIN and by adopting the law *on combating tax fraud and serious economic and financial crime* of 6 December 2013[79] .

---

[77] **TRACFIN and the fight against money laundering,** *Cour des Comptes annual public report, February 2012*
[78] Introduced by the Order of 30 January 2009 transposing the European Directive of 26 October 2005, the risk-based approach aims to encourage reporting professions to adapt their vigilance according to the level and intensity of the risks assessed at the time the customer relationship is established and throughout the customer's lifetime.
[79] This law, some of whose provisions were censured by the Constitutional Council in a decision on 4 December 2013,

The results were not long in coming: in 2013, the number of suspicious transaction reports received by TRACFIN increased by 6% compared with 2012[80] and by 33% in 2014 compared with 2013[81] , demonstrating the remarkable progress that has been made in the fight against money laundering. At the same time, TRACFIN also increased the number of investigations carried out into all these reports by 5%. These results can be explained in particular by an increase in reports of tax fraud and terrorist financing due to the national and international context.

All these factors demonstrate the effectiveness of the anti-money laundering system set up by the French authorities, but the work carried out by TRACFIN is only part of the system in place. The fight against money laundering is also organised by the administrative authorities responsible for regulating and supervising the banking and financial sector.

Section II: The administrative authorities responsible for regulating and supervising the banking and financial sector, the cornerstone of France's anti-money laundering system

The banking and financial sector, by virtue of its high volatility and the enormous stakes it represents at national and international economic level, is subject to permanent supervision by two competent administrative bodies: the Autorité de Contrôle Prudentiel et de Résolution, which is responsible for supervising banks, insurance companies and other persons falling within its remit, and the Autorité des Marchés Financiers, which, as its name suggests, specialises in the financial sector.

In the ongoing fight against money laundering, the specialist skills of such institutions are particularly valuable.

Following the 2008-2009 financial crisis, which had a major impact on the world's economic and financial systems, the French authorities decided to strengthen the organisation and management of the institutions responsible for regulating and supervising the banking and financial sector.

It was with this in mind that the Autorité de Contrôle Prudentiel (ACP) was created by decree on 21 January 2010, resulting from the merger of the Commission Bancaire, the Autorité de Contrôle des Assurances et Mutuelles (ACAM) and two licensing authorities, the Comité des Entreprises d'Assurance (CEA) and the Comité des Etablissements de Crédit et des Entreprises d'Investissement (CECEI). The merger of

---

aims in particular to broaden the powers of the tax authorities, which will be able to base their prosecutions on information obtained, regardless of its origin.

[80] **Fraud and money laundering: nearly 30,000 reports received by Tracfin in 2013,** 4 March 2014, *le Figaro*

[81] **Financial intelligence: TRACFIN's activity jumped 30% in 2014,** 16 April 2015, *l'Express*

these different bodies had already been envisaged as part of the *law on the modernisation of the economy of 4 August 2008*[82] , which authorised the French government to take such a decision, which in principle falls within the legislative domain, by means of ordinance, and had also been recommended by the *Deletré report of July 2009*[83] . It was finally under *the Banking Separation and Regulation Act of 26 July 2013* that the ACP was also given a role in preventing and resolving banking crises, becoming the Autorité de Contrôle Prudentiel et de Résolution (ACPR). This entity will take the form of an independent administrative authority attached to the Banque de France with its own financial autonomy, although it will not have legal personality (unlike the AMF), and its objective will be to ensure "the preservation of the stability of the financial system and the protection of customers, policyholders, members and beneficiaries of persons subject to its supervision[84] ".

The Autorité des Marchés Financiers (AMF), for its part, was founded long before by *the Financial Security Act of 1ᵉʳ August 2003* and is the result of the merger of several bodies: the Conseil des Marchés Financiers (CMF), the Commission des Opérations de Bourse (COB) and the Conseil de Discipline de la Gestion Financière (CDGF). By bringing these bodies together, the legislator wanted to enhance the visibility and effectiveness of regulation and supervision of the French financial centre through a single independent administrative authority with legal personality.

Its remit is set out in Article L621-1 of the CMF, which makes the AMF responsible for supervising financial markets, protecting and informing retail investors about their savings and financial investments, and regulating financial transactions. The AMF also has a duty to contribute to the regulation and harmonisation of the financial sector at European and international level.

Together with the AMF, the newly-formed ACPR now forms the two pillars of the *twin peaks*[85] model for supervising financial activities, with one body responsible for monitoring industry players and the other for ensuring compliance with professional obligations on financial markets.

In addition to their many roles, the ACPR and AMF are also responsible, under Article L561-36 of the CMF, for monitoring compliance with the French anti-money

---

[82] The merger was provided for in article 152 of the law of August 2008.

[83] The Deletré report was the result of a mission of reflection and proposals entrusted to the Inspectorate General of Finance (IGF) to improve the monitoring of compliance with professional obligations towards customers in the banking and financial sector.

[84] Provision set out in Article L612-1 of the CMF

[85] The regulation and supervision of the financial sector has two main objectives: prudential and the "proper conduct of business" through compliance with professional obligations towards customers. There are 4 models for implementing these objectives, *Twin Peaks* being one of them. Each objective is allocated to two different entities, which are then responsible for achieving them for the entire financial sector. The Twin Peaks model is also applied by Australia and the Netherlands.

laundering provisions of the same code and the *Regulation of 20 May 2015 on information accompanying transfers of funds* to persons subject to its supervision. The ACPR is therefore responsible for the professionals listed in Article L612-2 of the CMF (credit institutions, insurance companies, etc.), while the AMF is responsible for the industry players listed in Article L561-36 grand I 2°) of the CMF (portfolio management companies, financial investment advisers, etc.).

The main role of these two bodies is to ensure that regulated professionals comply with two obligations: an obligation of constant vigilance based on a risk-based approach involving analytical work, and an obligation to report suspicions to TRACFIN, this time based on pragmatic work.

To this end, the ACPR and the AMF have special powers enabling them to carry out off-site inspections, with the right to request any useful document or information, or on-site inspections on the premises where the business is carried out by specially authorised inspectors. They also have the right to obtain any document they need to carry out their duties from government departments, local authorities, public establishments and any person entrusted with a public service remit.

If, in the course of their duties, they observe one or more breaches of the anti-money laundering rules by one of the persons subject to their supervision, the Sanctions Committee of the ACPR or the AMF (depending on the professional accused of the breach) will then have jurisdiction and will apply one of the sanctions provided for in Articles L612-39 et seq. of the CMF, which may range from a simple warning to total withdrawal of authorisation[86] or removal from the register of insurance intermediaries[87].

In line with this mission, the ACPR's Collège de Supervision[88] decided on 28 May 2010 to set up *an anti-money laundering advisory committee to* assist the Collège in its decision-making on anti-money laundering issues. Prior to the adoption of any decision relating to the fight against money laundering, the committee will be asked to issue an opinion.

The originality of this committee lies in its composition, which is made up of professionals subject to ACPR supervision, representatives of banking and insurance industry associations and a representative of the Caisse des Dépôts et de Consignation, all chaired by two members of the Board. Through this committee, the ACPR has access to feedback from industry professionals and is thus aware of the

---

[86] This mainly concerns banks and financial institutions.

[87] This mainly concerns insurance brokers, general agents and authorised agents.

[88] The Supervisory Board is the decision-making body of the ACPR, which acts in different configurations depending on the subject to be dealt with

practical problems they encounter on a day-to-day basis, thus ensuring that decisions are taken in line with economic and financial reality. The Director of TRACFIN, the Treasury Directorate General and the Director of the CNIL[89] are also invited to take part in the committee's deliberations when matters concerning them are being examined, and can therefore contribute their expertise to the committee's work.

Alongside these two authorities, a decree of 18 January 2010 established *the Conseil d'Orientation de la Lutte contre le Laundering de capitaux et le Financement du Terrorisme* (COLB), an informal coordination body made up of all government departments and supervisory authorities involved in the fight against money laundering.

Meeting on a quarterly basis, the COLB seeks solutions to improve and strengthen the national system, and also aims to raise awareness among regulated professionals of their obligations to exercise due diligence and report suspicious transactions, as well as of the challenges involved in combating money laundering.

Lastly, the ACPR and AMF also play an important role at international level. In February 2012, the ACPR contributed to the FATF's work on revising the *40 Recommendations, as well as* at European level, where it participates in *the Anti Money Laundering Committee* (AMLC)[90] .

The AMF is a member of the International Organisation of Securities Commissions (IOSCO), where it represents France in the harmonisation of financial market rules, including anti-money laundering measures, and participates in the drafting of international recommendations based on FATF standards. At EU level, the AMF is regularly invited to contribute its expertise to the definition of standards aimed at transposing within the EU the principles developed by IOSCO and other international organisations specialising in financial regulation[91] .

To date, the tasks entrusted to the supervisory and regulatory authorities by the anti-money laundering mechanism appear to have been implemented, with the latter carrying out regular monitoring, which is then the subject of an annual report sent to the Director of the ACPR and the AMF.

The controls put in place show that, on the whole, anti-money laundering measures are being applied satisfactorily by regulated professionals, although there are still shortcomings in terms of staff training, the implementation of a permanent and

---

[89] The Commission Nationale de l'Informatique et des Libertés (CNIL) is an independent administrative authority that ensures that information technology does not harm individuals.

[90] The AMLC is an anti-money laundering think tank attached to the Joint Committee of the three European financial sector authorities: the European Banking Authority (EBA), the European Insurance and Occupational Pensions Authority (EIOPA) and the European Securities and Markets Authority (ESMA).

[91] These include the Financial Stability Board and the Joint Forum of the Basel Committee.

periodic internal control system and the collection of detailed information on customers, particularly in the area of wealth management, a sector considered to be a priority due to the large number of foreign customers domiciled in countries where the fight against money laundering is still inadequate[92] .

The establishment of such an anti-money laundering system by the French public authorities, influenced by the recommendations issued at international level and made mandatory by Community law, was not an easy task. Administrative departments had to be created or expanded to meet the requirements of the fight against money laundering and, more recently, against the financing of terrorism.

But such measures have also led to a real upheaval in the professional practice of the economic, financial and even legal agents concerned, who have had to rethink the organisation and conception of their profession with a view to participating effectively in the necessary fight against money laundering.

---

[92] **Report on on-site inspections of compliance with LCB-FT obligations in the field of asset management for the banking and insurance sectors,** February 2012, *ACPR report.*

CHAPTER 2

Application of the anti-money laundering provisions to economic and legal agents directly or indirectly exposed to money laundering networks

The fight against money laundering and the financing of terrorism is a long and tedious battle, both for the specialised national and international bodies, which have to be as creative or more creative than the money launderers in developing their standards, since money laundering techniques are constantly being updated, and for the professionals, who have to comply meticulously with all these measures or risk being penalised.

Implementing these measures was a real headache for many of them, as professionals had to strike a perfect balance between the need for compliance, the operability of the system and maintaining future commercial prospects. Despite all the parameters to be taken into consideration, implementation was necessary and had to be carried out fairly quickly, in order to comply with the European directives and the national laws adopted as a result.

The system established at the time by the French authorities imposed a series of obligations on regulated professionals with a view to effectively combating money laundering **(A),** but although it is effective, it nevertheless raises a number of questions **(B)**.

A) The French anti-money laundering system

The obligations imposed on players in the banking and financial sector have continued to multiply and strengthen since 1987[93] , the date of France's first anti-money laundering law, which transformed a duty specific to credit institutions, mainly concerning the declaration of sums appearing to derive from drug trafficking[94] , into a collective necessity now affecting the entire banking and financial sector as well as certain legal professions.

Indeed, the involvement of these sectors was essential, as they were an almost indispensable element in the laundering operations of criminal organisations. What's more, with financial transactions now being exchanged around the world so rapidly and in such colossal volumes, it was becoming increasingly difficult for the authorities

---

[93] Cf. above P. 33

[94] Provided for in *the Act of 12 July 1990 relating to the participation of financial institutions in the fight against the laundering of money derived from drug trafficking.*

to detect money laundering schemes disguised as operations that were extremely difficult to identify.

Other factors also necessitated this involvement, such as the change in customer consumption patterns leading to the rise of online banking and the success of investment funds. Another important factor that contributed to the mobilisation of these sectors was the resurgence of complex corporate structures, such as trusts or shell companies, within which it is very difficult to identify the constituents, particularly in tax havens. Taken together, these factors undoubtedly lead to a high level of financial opacity, which is proving to be a panacea for criminal organisations. The danger posed by money laundering also appears immense in view of the systemic risk it could cause, particularly by destabilising the equilibrium of the financial markets. The incessant exchange of 'dirty' money could seriously damage the reputation of banking and financial establishments and the credibility of the markets, which are based entirely on a system of trust between investors and institutions, ultimately leading to the collapse of the system. The introduction of an anti-money laundering system is therefore justified, over and above the traditional desire to dismantle criminal organisations, by this important underlying economic issue.

However, the development of such a system, while fundamental, cannot be sufficient on its own, as its effectiveness depends essentially on full cooperation between the various players involved at both national and international level. It is with this in mind that France has sought to establish the necessary cooperation between its supervisory authorities, its financial intelligence unit and the professionals operating in the sectors subject to the system.

The legislator was therefore faced with a real challenge in that it had to involve these professionals in the fight against money laundering by putting in place a system which, while imposing obligations on them, would not unnecessarily harm their business practices or penalise them unfairly.

In the light of all these factors, the legislator has drawn up a series of measures in the form of numerous laws, whether or not transposing European directives, while bearing in mind the need to strike a balance between the fight against money laundering and the maintenance of a healthy business in the sectors concerned.

The first law to introduce such a system was *the law of 12 July 1990 on the participation of financial institutions in the fight against the laundering of money derived from drug trafficking*, which already laid down certain obligations for credit institutions and the financial professions. These already included the obligation to report to the newly established TRACFIN any sums entered in their books that appeared to derive from drug trafficking, as well as any transactions involving such sums. The law also laid down a whole series of provisions relating to customer identification and the duty of vigilance that professionals had to respect throughout the business relationship. This text thus laid the foundations for all the legislative work that followed, drawn up in accordance with the European anti-money laundering directives adopted at Community level.

Today, the scope of the anti-money laundering mechanism has been considerably extended by the legislator's extensive legislative output, which now involves all players in the banking and financial sector, as well as certain legal professions.

The professionals subject to anti-money laundering obligations are listed in Article L561-2 of the Monetary and Financial Code, which was issued by *the Order of 30 January 2009 on the prevention of the use of the financial system for the purpose of money laundering and terrorist financing*[95] . The entire banking and financial sector is listed in this article, as well as certain legal professions considered likely to be exposed to money laundering, such as lawyers[96] . It should be noted that with the meteoric rise of Crowdfunding, advisers and intermediaries in participative investment are also subject to the obligations of the anti-money laundering scheme following *the Order of 30 May 2014 on participative financing.*

The anti-money laundering system thus established sets out two types of obligations that must be scrupulously complied with by regulated professionals, namely a duty of vigilance with regard to customers **(Section I)** and a duty to report suspicions to TRACFIN **(Section II).** These obligations represent a real challenge, as any breach may result in the professional being held liable **(Section III).**

Section I: Customer due diligence

The Second European Anti-Money Laundering Directive of 4 December 2001 had already required Member States to introduce a "threshold" approach to vigilance for banks and financial institutions. Under this method, regulated professionals were obliged to request information from their customers as soon as they carried out transactions exceeding a certain amount, i.e. €15,000[97] .

However, this approach was widely criticised by the banking and financial sector,

---

[95] It should be noted that almost all of the current anti-money laundering provisions derive from or were amended by the Order of 30 July 2009, subject to certain subsequent amendments. The purpose of this Order was to transpose the European Union's Third Money Laundering Directive of 26 October 2005. This Order has now been replaced by the Order of 1er December 2016, transposing the Fourth European Directive of 2015.

[96] In this A, we will deal mainly with the banking and financial sectors, which are at the forefront of the fight against money laundering. However, the legal professions referred to in Article L561-2 of the CMF are, with a few exceptions, subject to the same obligations and will be dealt with in more detail in section B.

[97] The threshold was different for life insurance policies, with customer identification becoming compulsory once the amount of premiums paid annually exceeded €1,000.

which felt that it did not reflect reality. Using the "smurfing" technique ([98]), criminal organisations could continue to launder the proceeds of their crimes without exceeding the vigilance thresholds. Conversely, some perfectly "clean" companies used to carrying out large transactions were constantly and unjustifiably placed under surveillance.

The Third European Anti-Money Laundering Directive of 26 October 2005 took these considerations into account by establishing a new "risk-based" approach, this time based on an assessment of the real risk of money laundering. The assessment of the degree of vigilance by the banker or financial institution will no longer be based on the amount of transactions carried out by the customer, but on his personal profile, the products used or simply his "banking habits".

This directive was transposed by the 2009 Order, which codified the "risk-based" approach to due diligence in a new section 3, *"Customer Due Diligence"*[99], which is part of the chapter on the fight against money laundering and terrorist financing in the Monetary and Financial Code. The decree of 2 September 2009 subsequently specified the conditions for applying the new provisions.

Today, new European anti-money laundering legislation has progressively strengthened this obligation, culminating in the latest order of 1er December 2016 transposing the Vème directive.

The obligation of vigilance thus laid down must be applied consistently by the professional to a greater or lesser degree, adapted according to three degrees **(§1). It is** with a view to this adaptation that perfect knowledge of the customer is essential **(§2).**

§1 *Different levels of customer vigilance*

The Monetary and Financial Code identifies various types of customer, who are classified according to three levels of vigilance depending on the money laundering risk they represent.

The first level of due diligence introduced by the Order is **simplified or light due diligence** and is provided for in article L561-9 of the Monetary and Financial Code. Since this type of due diligence is characterised by the fact that the customer, the services requested or the products used present a low risk of money laundering, the provisions applicable during the business relationship[100] can be implemented in a simplified manner. In addition, the implementation of this level of vigilance must be

---

[98] Cf. above P. 7

[99] The obligation to exercise due diligence is set out in articles L561-4-1 to L561-14-2 of the CMF, some of which have been amended by subsequent legislation.

[100] Articles L561-5 and L561-6 of the Monetary and Financial Code, respectively.

justified to the ACPR.

Under article L561-9 II of the Monetary and Financial Code, the 2009 Order offered the possibility of a total exemption from the obligations incumbent on professionals in several cases. The new Order of 2016, aimed at transposing the Vème directive, reduced the scope of this exemption. At the time, it was stipulated that, depending on the profile of the customer or the product concerned, the exemption would apply automatically. Today, a new condition has been added, namely that the customer must not be suspected of money laundering. The professional must therefore meet this double condition in order to be exempted from his obligation of vigilance. The CMF has therefore introduced two sets of circumstances in which this exemption applies.

The first set of cases, defined by Article R561-15 of the CMF, is assessed on the basis of the customer's profile and concerns :

- banking and financial institutions established in France, in a Member State of the European Union, in a State party to the Agreement on the European Economic Area or in a third country with an equivalent anti-money laundering system
- Listed companies whose shares are admitted to trading on at least one regulated market in France or in a State party to the Agreement on the European Economic Area.
- Public authorities or bodies whose identity is transparent and certain, and whose activities are transparent and subject to appropriate control procedures

The second series of cases, this time provided for in article R561-16, concerns the types of transactions exempting the professional from his duty of vigilance. There are eleven of these, including life insurance contracts where the annual premium paid does not exceed €1,000[101] or where the single premium does not exceed €2,500, and consumer credit not exceeding €1,000 and meeting various conditions.

Of course, the professional must gather a certain amount of information about the customer in order to assess their profile before they can benefit from this exemption[102].

Finally, it should be noted that the specific cases of exemption from the insurance due diligence obligation are expressly provided for in the Order of 10 November 2009.

The second level provides for **normal vigilance where there is** a medium risk of money laundering, and therefore concerns the vast majority of customers. In this

---

[101] In the case of life insurance, the threshold of €1,000 used for the previous approach to due diligence has been retained.

[102] Provision set out in Article R561-17 of the CMF

case, articles L561-5 and L561-6 of the CMF are fully applicable at the time the relationship is established and throughout the relationship[103] .

The final level, **that of enhanced vigilance**, applies when the risk of money laundering and/or terrorist financing is highest, as provided for in articles L561-10-1 to L561-10-3 of the CMF:

- Cross-border correspondent banking relationships[104] or business relationships with a view to distributing financial instruments with a foreign financial institution located in a country that is not a member of the European Union, that is not party to an agreement on the European Economic Area or that does not have an equivalent anti-money laundering system.

  In such a case, article L561-10-3 of the CMF provides for the implementation of standard due diligence obligations and refers to the implementing decree, which sets out the enhanced measures to be implemented with regard to the foreign institution, such as the assessment of the anti-money laundering system applied by the institution or the gathering of information about the institution relating to the nature of its activities or its reputation.

- Transactions that appear to be extremely complex, of unusually high value or that appear to have no economic justification or lawful purpose.

  When faced with this type of transaction, professionals are obliged to carry out an enhanced scrutiny by obtaining information directly from the customer on the origin or destination of the funds, the purpose of the transaction and the identity of the beneficiary. To this end, banking and financial institutions must establish internal procedures detailing the information to be gathered, a non-exhaustive list of which was provided by the AMF in its guidelines of 15 March 2010[105] . As part of this enhanced review, it is recommended that the characteristics of the transaction and the identity of those likely to be interested in its implementation in terms of remuneration be gathered. Once this analysis has been completed, the professional must file a report with TRACFIN under article L561-15 III° if he has not managed to eliminate the suspicion.

- The last case of enhanced due diligence, provided for by article L561-10-3 paragraph 2 of the CMF, is not an obligation on the part of the professional but

---

[103] With regard to traditional due diligence obligations, see P. 53 below.

[104] *Correspondent banking is* the practice whereby a bank uses another foreign credit institution to receive payments or services in foreign currency. This practice is based on the principle that a national currency cannot leave its country of origin.

[105] **AMF guidelines clarifying certain provisions of the General Regulation on the prevention of money laundering and terrorist financing,** 15 March 2010, AMF

a prohibition. This provision prohibits the establishment or maintenance of a cross-border correspondent banking relationship with a financial institution based in a country where the latter has no effective physical presence. Similarly, paragraph 3 requires regulated persons to ensure that they do not maintain a business relationship with a person who is himself connected with an institution of this type.

The aim of this provision is to rule out any relationship with institutions that could serve as front companies for criminal organisations, since such arrangements could enable the latter to channel 'dirty' money through French financial institutions.

Article L561-10 of the Monetary and Financial Code sets out a final series of so-called **additional due diligence** measures, which apply to professionals in addition to the traditional due diligence obligations (L561-5 to L561-6) in the following cases:

- The customer or their legal representative is not physically present at the time of identification, which is particularly common with the growing success of online banking.
- The customer is a politically exposed person (PEP)[106] or has strong friendly or family ties with a PEP. A list of such persons is set out in article R561-18 of the CMF, including heads of state and government and senior military officials.
- The transaction or product envisaged favours customer anonymity, which essentially refers to anonymous bonds and securities and transactions relating thereto in accordance with Article R561-19 of the CMF.
- All transactions on your own account or on behalf of third parties with natural or legal persons established in a country on the FATF's "black list".

These additional due diligence measures are set out in article R561-20 of the CMF and include obtaining additional supporting documents to confirm the identity of the customer, certification of the said official documents by an expert, the requirement to make an initial payment to or from a person holding an account with an institution located in a Member State or any State party to the EEA Agreement, and confirmation of the customer's identity by one of the aforementioned institutions. The law stipulates that at least two of these measures must be carried out by the professional in one of the aforementioned cases.

All of these provisions set out in the 2016 Order constitute the minimum obligations necessary to combat money laundering. However, professionals will be free to define their own internal risk management policy in order to tailor controls to the customer's

---

[106] PPE, Cf. below P. 56

profile. This internal policy must also comply with article R561-38 of the CMF, which sets out the conditions for application of the risk assessment and management system.

It is clear from these provisions that the main thrust of these due diligence obligations is to ensure that customers are effectively known by regularly updating information about them. This requirement corresponds to the *Know Your Customer* (KYC) principle.

§2 *The essential application of the KYC principle*

The concept of KYC was initially established by the FATF and consists of a set of measures to be applied by banking and financial institutions in order to have a perfect knowledge of the customer and thus detect transactions that do not correspond to the customer's profile. This concept has gradually been extended to other professions subject to anti-money laundering measures.

This knowledge of the customer must therefore traditionally be acquired in two stages, firstly at the time the business relationship is entered into **(a)** and then throughout the relationship **(b)**, although certain specific cases do not fit into this classic process **(c).**

a) *Due diligence obligations when entering into a relationship*

Article L561-5 of the CMF sets out the obligations to be met when entering into a relationship with a customer, and therefore before any assistance is given in preparing or carrying out a financial transaction. Under this article, professionals are responsible for effectively identifying customers by obtaining various documentary evidence, regardless of their status (natural persons, legal entities or other banking or financial institutions). They must also identify the purpose and nature of the business relationship that the customer wishes to establish.

Professionals subject to this obligation will have to carry out a series of checks provided for in article R561-5 of the CMF, when the customer is a natural person, relating to his identity, any powers of attorney of his representative(s) and his address, the latter being verified by means of the "welcome letter[107] ". Banking and financial institutions will also ask for any documents that can be used to determine the customer's profile based on their economic situation. Determining the customer's profile will be essential in assessing the transactions carried out by the customer, since the professional will be able to assess whether the transactions correspond to

---

[107] The practice used by banking and financial institutions of sending a letter of greeting to the address given by the customer at the time the relationship is established. This letter has to be returned to the institution for some reason, and it is only by sending it back that the institution can confirm that the address given is correct.

the customer's economic capacity or whether they appear suspicious.

However, there is a qualification to this measure, set out in IV° of article L561-5 of the CMF, where the risk of money laundering appears to be low from the outset. In such cases, professionals are authorised to identify the customer during the establishment of the business relationship. However, this provision can only be applied in the four cases listed exhaustively in Article R561-6 of the CMF:
- Opening an account
- The conclusion of a contract, provided that the professional can justify to the supervisory authority the low risk of money laundering and the need to continue the business relationship that has already begun
- Taking out an insurance policy
- Transactions relating to the financing of physical assets where ownership is not transferred or is only transferred at the end of the contractual relationship (essentially leasing contracts).

It should be noted that the identification must also concern the beneficial owner of this business relationship, defined by article L561-2-2 of the CMF as "the natural person who directly or indirectly controls the customer, or the person for whom a transaction is executed or an activity carried out". Article R561-1 of the CMF provides some clarification in cases where the customer is a legal entity.

It considers the beneficial owner to be the natural person(s) holding, directly or indirectly, at least 25% of the capital or voting rights of the client company or exercising a controlling, administrative or management power within the company or the general meeting.

Once this information has been obtained, the banking or financial institution will draw up a customer profile to determine the degree of vigilance applicable to the customer and may be exempted from its obligations if the risk of money laundering appears low under article L561-9 II of the CMF.

Only once these steps have been taken will the banking or financial institution be able to enter into a business relationship consisting of "a professional or commercial relationship which, at the time the contact is established, is expected to last for a certain period of time", under the terms of article L561-2-1 of the CMF.

b) <u>Due diligence obligations applicable during the business relationship</u>

Article L561-6 of the CMF imposes due diligence obligations on professionals throughout the relationship, requiring "constant vigilance and careful examination of transactions carried out, ensuring that they are consistent with their up-to-date knowledge of their customer".

Specifying how these obligations are to be applied, the Order of 2 September 2009 stipulates that, to this end, the banking or financial institution must clearly identify the amount and nature of the transactions envisaged, the source and destination of the funds as well as the economic justification declared by the customer or the envisaged operation of the account, in order to have full knowledge of the account. The study of these various elements will also enable professionals to determine the nature of the business relationship, as envisaged in article R561-12.

This is why the constant updating of customer information is very important for taxable persons, since they will be able to assess whether the degree of vigilance initially applied still corresponds to the risk presented by the customer throughout the relationship.

Article R561-11 of the CMF also provides for cases where banking or financial institutions "have good reason to believe that the identity of their customer and the identification details previously obtained are no longer accurate or relevant". In this situation, the law requires professionals to re-identify the customer and analyse any changes, however minor, that are likely to alter the customer's risk profile. They will have to examine any changes in the customer's professional situation or address, or whether the customer has become a PEP during the course of the relationship. Similarly, if the customer is a legal entity, it will be necessary to examine any changes in status or location, among other things. Every aspect of the due diligence process is therefore important, and nothing should be left to chance.

c) *Specific obligations applicable to particular cases*

By their very nature, certain types of customer lead banking and financial institutions to apply specific measures. These include politically exposed persons.

The PEP is a concept originally defined by the FATF in its Recommendation No. 12 as "persons who hold or have held important public positions, for example, Heads of State and Government, senior politicians, senior government officials, senior members of the judiciary and the military, heads of state-owned enterprises, senior members of political parties or senior officials of international organisations". In including this category of persons in the fight against money laundering, the FATF assumed that the EPP's former political responsibility could make them susceptible to being linked to various corruption cases.

The concept of the PEP was taken up by the European anti-money laundering directives, which were gradually transposed into national law. The PEP was then included in the cases of additional vigilance set out in article L561-10 of the CMF. A list of persons who qualify as PEPs is provided in article R561-18.

It should be noted, however, that nationals who have carried out such activities have been included in the scope of PEPs since the IVème European Directive, based on the recent revision of the FATF *40 Recommendations* of February 2012. However, this extension did not come as a surprise, as the French supervisory authorities had already been recommending since 2013[108] that professionals take account of the revision of recommendation 12, which included national PEPs.

Article R561-20 II° sets out specific provisions to be applied to PPEs in parallel to those set out in R561-20 I°. Professionals must therefore :

- Apply a risk management system to determine whether the customer is a PEP
- Obtain authorisation from a member of the institution's executive body to enter into contact with the PPE
- Research the origin of the funds and assets involved in the business relationship

In addition to the provisions set out in the CMF, the AMF issued a position paper in 2013[109] stating that, in the case of business relationships with customers linked to third countries with non-equivalent anti-money laundering provisions or countries identified as having high levels of corruption and/or organised crime, it is necessary to check whether the customer's beneficial owner is a PEP or presents a high risk of money laundering.

Professionals subject to the law may also be faced with the problem of unidentifiable customers.

Article L561-8 of the CMF provides for a situation where the banking or financial institution is unable to identify its customer or to obtain information about the purpose and nature of the proposed business relationship. In such cases, the professional must not carry out any transaction or establish any business relationship. This obligation also applies when a business relationship has been entered into where there is a low risk of money laundering (article L561-5 IV°) and requires the relationship to be terminated.

Thus, when the professional is obliged to terminate the business relationship with the customer under article L561-8 of the CMF, he must file a suspicious transaction report with TRACFIN if he suspects or has good reason to believe that a money laundering offence has been committed. This reporting obligation is the second duty of professionals subject to the anti-money laundering provisions.

---

[108] This recommendation was made in the same *AMF position-recommendation of 2013* and *in the ACPR's updated guidelines of 12 November 2013*.

[109] Guidelines on the concept of politically exposed persons in the fight against money laundering and terrorist financing of 13 February 2013, *AMF Position-Recommendation No. 2013-23*.

Reporting suspicious transactions is one of the key points in the fight against money laundering, since it is only by making these reports that the Financial Intelligence Unit can investigate and _ultimately_ enable the authorities to combat these clandestine networks.

Recommendation 20 of the FATF[110] , known as the "_suspicious transaction report_", states that "if a financial institution suspects or has reasonable grounds to suspect that funds are derived from criminal activity or are related to the financing of terrorism, it should be required, directly by law or regulation, to file a suspicious transaction report with the financial intelligence unit without delay".

Although the practice already existed in French law since the 1990 law, the concept of reporting suspicious transactions was reinforced by the European anti-money laundering directives before being transposed into French law. Apart from the COSI automated system[111] , France does not use early warning software and has developed a system based on the analysis of each sum or transaction in the light of the customer's risk profile and the institution's classification policy.

If, as a result of this analysis, a money laundering offence is found to have been committed or if there are suspicions that it may have been committed, the regulated professional must file a suspicious transaction report with TRACFIN.

The duty to report suspicions is set out in Articles L561-15 to L561-22-1 of Section IV of the chapter on obligations relating to the fight against money laundering and terrorist financing of the CMF. The scope of application of this provision remains unchanged, with Article L561-15 still referring to regulated professionals under Article L561-2 of the CMF.

However, the introduction of such an obligation may legitimately raise questions about the concept of suspicion, which has not been defined by the legislator. Some authors have attempted to provide a definition, one of which considers that it is "_an anomaly in a transaction that should attract attention, not because it is in itself abnormal, but because a certain number of objective, precise and verifiable signs or indications do not correspond to what the professional knows about his co-contractor. Suspicion is therefore always the result of an irreconcilable confrontation, carried out in concreto, between the transaction in question and the client's ordinary practices_".[112]

---

[110] Initially included in recommendation 13, the "suspicious transaction report" has been included in recommendation 20 since the 2012 revision.

[111] Systematic communication of information Cf. P.28

[112] **The metamorphoses of French anti-money laundering legislation,** _Fabrice Defferrard,_ **Gazette du Palais 23 and 24 October 2009**

The duty to declare must be fulfilled when the professional is confronted with a transaction falling within its scope **(§1),** but once the declaration has been made, the professional is still bound by various obligations, failure to comply with which could result in liability **(§2).**

§1 *The scope of the reporting obligation*

The material scope of the reporting obligation has expanded considerably in recent years under the impetus of the European anti-money laundering directives. Article L561-15 I° of the CMF now stipulates that regulated professions must report "sums entered in their books or transactions involving sums which they know, suspect or have good reason to suspect originate from an offence punishable by a custodial sentence of more than one year or are involved in the financing of terrorism".

By way of comparison, the former article L561-15 of the *Act of 5 March 2007 on the prevention of delinquency* covered only five offences[113] whereas the article in its current form now includes offences punishable by a custodial sentence of more than 1 year since the 2009 Order, i.e. virtually the entire Penal Code with the exception of minor offences. In this way, the laundering of the proceeds of offences such as fraud, breach of trust or misuse of corporate assets must now be reported to TRACFIN, but the real aim of the 2009 Order was to include the laundering of tax fraud within the scope of application. This objective is clearly stated in the letter of Article L561-15 II°, which expressly provides for the reporting of suspicions of tax fraud.

Under the terms of Article 1741 of the General Tax Code, tax fraud consists of the fraudulent evasion or attempted evasion by a person of all or part of the assessment or payment of tax, and is punishable by five years' imprisonment and a fine of 500,000 euros, regardless of the applicable tax penalties and in the absence of aggravating circumstances[114] .

This offence can be committed in a number of ways, and article D561-32-1 of the CMF, issued by the decree of 2 September 2009, provides a list of sixteen criteria enabling regulated professionals to determine whether they are faced with an attempt to launder tax fraud.

These include, in particular, the use of shell companies carrying out an activity that is not in line with their corporate purpose, the frequent deposit or withdrawal of cash on a business account that is not justified by the level or nature of the economic

---

[113] The material scope of the reporting obligation includes sums or transactions that may be the proceeds of drug trafficking, fraud against the financial interests of the European Communities, corruption, organised criminal activity or that may contribute to the financing of terrorism.

[114] Conviction for tax fraud can be increased to seven years' imprisonment and a fine of €3,000,000 where the offences were committed by an organised gang or facilitated by various means.

activity, or the carrying out of financial transactions that are inconsistent or suspicious in relation to the company's usual activities in sectors that are sensitive to VAT fraud of the carousel type[115].

Of course, the criteria defined in Article D561-32-1 of the CMF are not exhaustive, in that other situations not listed in the text may also constitute tax fraud. These are merely "indicators". Conversely, the text refers to situations where there is a strong presumption of fraud but which do not constitute evidence of possible tax fraud. The legislator's intention with this article was in fact to give impetus to future suspicious transaction reports relating to tax fraud, newly introduced into the scope of application of L561-15 of the CMF, even if it meant setting criteria that were perhaps a little too broad.

Paragraph IV of Article L561-15 of the CMF covers the case of supplementary declarations enabling a professional to complete or amend a previous declaration to TRACFIN.

The significance of this paragraph lies in a provision added by *the Act of 26 July 2013 on the separation and regulation of banking activities,* under which all attempts at money laundering or tax fraud must now also be reported to TRACFIN by means of a suspicious transaction report. Attempted money laundering is defined as any practice aimed at concealing the proceeds of an offence (tax, crime, misdemeanour) that has not been completed. This provision shows the extent of the mechanism put in place to combat money launderers.

Another important obligation for professionals is the implementation of the COSI system[116] under article L561-15-1 of the CMF. Under this provision, banking and financial institutions must systematically send TRACFIN information on transactions presenting a high risk of money laundering or terrorist financing because of the countries involved, their nature or the legal structures concerned.

The decree of 23 March 2015, in article R561-31-2 of the Monetary and Financial Code, sets out the conditions for applying this provision and the threshold at which the COSI must be activated. It is now stipulated that cash deposits and withdrawals made on an account or via a customer's account, the cumulative amount of which exceeds 10,000 euros over a calendar month, must be systematically reported via the COSI system.

This means that TRACFIN has access to the monthly bank details of any customer

---

[115] Carousel fraud is a complex form of VAT fraud involving several companies established in at least two EU Member States. The fraud consists of obtaining a reduction or refund of the VAT relating to an intra-Community supply of goods when this VAT has not been paid to the Treasury.
[116] Systematic Information Communication System, Cf. P. 28

exceeding this threshold, even if the customer has never been involved in any money laundering offence. Although this provision may seem dubious in terms of the right to privacy, it should be pointed out that this information will not be analysed by TRACFIN, but will simply be added to its STARTRAC database. Furthermore, if a customer who has already been the subject of a COSI is concerned by a suspicious transaction report, TRACFIN will be able to re-use the information acquired under Article L561-15-1 of the CMF.

Once a professional has made a declaration in one of these cases, he or she is not free to do so. The French Monetary and Financial Code sets out a number of obligations that professionals must meet, or risk being held liable.

§2 *The professional's obligations after the declaration*

Once a professional has reported suspicions, the anti-money laundering rules set out a series of obligations to ensure that they do not hinder the work of TRACFIN.

These include the obligation to report the suspicious transaction before it is carried out, as set out in Article L561-16 paragraph 1er , in order to allow TRACFIN to exercise its blocking powers while it examines the report.

Under Article L561-24 of the CMF, the French FIU has the power to block a suspicious transaction while it examines the corresponding declarations sent by the professional. The professional must be notified of the transaction freeze, which may not last more than ten working days from the date of notification. However, the period may be extended by a further ten days by decision of the President of the Paris Tribunal de Grande Instance.

In addition, if the transaction was carried out before the report was made for any reason whatsoever, the trader must send the report to TRACFIN[117] without delay.

To the same end, the Monetary and Financial Code imposes a real obligation of confidentiality on the professional with regard to the declaration made. This obligation is set out in article L561-18 and failure to comply may result in a fine of 22,500 euros being imposed on the person making the disclosure under article L574-1 of the CMF.

The particular case referred to here is the possible warning about the proceedings in progress that the professional might give to his client, although the article specifies that the fact that a lawyer seeks to convince his client not to take part in such activities does not fall within the scope of this sanction.

---

[117] The law provides for three cases in which the transaction may have been carried out prior to the report being made, namely the impossibility of postponing its execution, the possibility that the postponement could harm ongoing investigations and the appearance of the suspicion after the transaction.

This suspicious transaction report is therefore only available to TRACFIN. Only TRACFIN's referral to the Public Prosecutor will enable the judicial authorities to have knowledge of the report, except in the specific case where the report is requested by the Public Prosecutor in order to institute criminal proceedings against regulated professionals if investigations have revealed their involvement in money laundering offences.

However, Article L561-20 of the CMF amends this duty of confidentiality between regulated professionals. Under this article, they are authorised to disclose the existence and content of this declaration to other professionals belonging to the same group, network or professional structure. In addition, these professionals must also be subject to the reporting obligations and be based either in France or in a country with an equivalent anti-money laundering system. Similarly, such disclosure may only be made for the purpose of combating money laundering and the financing of terrorism.

Lastly, Article L561-22 of the CMF introduces an important element of the duty to report suspicions, namely exemption from criminal and civil liability for regulated professionals, supervisory authorities (essentially the President of the Bar for lawyers) or any person who has provided information to TRACFIN in good faith. However, IV° of this article imposes a twofold condition on this exemption: the professional must have made the declaration under the conditions set out in Articles L561-16 to L561-24 of the CMF and must not have colluded fraudulently with the customer.

The introduction of such an anti-money laundering system very quickly became a crucial issue for banking and financial institutions, given that the supervisory authorities, the ACPR and the AMF, conscientiously monitor compliance with vigilance and reporting obligations, as well as the implementation of an internal policy designed to effectively combat money laundering.

Consequently, any failure by these establishments to comply with their professional obligations, without necessarily having caused any malfunction, is likely to result in the application of both administrative and disciplinary sanctions.

Section III: Proper application of the anti-money laundering provisions: a major challenge for regulated professionals.

With the progressive strengthening of the anti-money laundering measures, failure to comply with these obligations can be a dangerous game with serious consequences.

As part of their supervisory role, the supervisory authorities have the power to impose sanctions in the event of non-compliance with anti-money laundering measures.

These penalties are far from insignificant, since they range from a warning to removal of the establishment from the list of approved persons, and may also be accompanied by publication and a substantial financial penalty.

Based on the case law of the ACPR's Sanctions Committee, the most common sanctions are fines of between €70,000 and €500,000, usually accompanied by a reprimand[118] . These decisions are often taken in response to various failings on the part of professionals to comply with the obligations set out in the anti-money laundering provisions, namely failure to report suspicious transactions or delays in doing so, poor application of vigilance or KYC obligations, a lack of technical and human resources allocated to the system or simply poor organisation of the institution's risk detection procedures.

In addition to disciplinary convictions, regulated professionals may also be exposed to criminal sanctions when their breaches are classified as complicity in money laundering or concealment of money laundering. Of course, as is the rule in criminal law, these acts must be committed intentionally, which in practice seems to limit the application of such convictions to banking and financial institutions.

However, most authors do not seem to be definitive on this issue, as some consider that the criminal court "*will make an assessment in abstracto to determine whether, for example, the banker, in accordance with a diligent and competent reference prototype, would have concluded that this was possible on the basis of information that he would have had, or that he would have obtained by fulfilling the obligations of vigilance[119]* ". This would mean that judges would base themselves on the obligations set out in the anti-money laundering provisions in order to determine whether or not the element of intent was present, taking the view that compliance with these obligations would constitute the benchmark for determining whether the professional acted in good or bad faith.

However, such an interpretation could prove to be double-edged, as professionals would seek to benefit from the exemption from criminal liability and would multiply the number of declarations in cases that do not necessarily require it. In this way, sending multiple declarations could tend to clog up TRACFIN's investigation departments.

For the time being, there is no case law in which a regulated professional has been convicted of money laundering, so this aspect of liability remains illusory. Furthermore, with a view to optimising the anti-money laundering system, it is highly

---

[118] ACPR Sanctions Committee decisions: **Auxiliaire Parisienne de services financiers,** *5 February 2013* or **Banque Populaire Côte d'Azur,** *10 January 2013*

[119] **Aspect pénal des obligations de vigilance tendant à prévenir le blanchiment,** *Philippe Conte,* **JCP G 2005**

likely that the public authorities will seek to step up controls and, consequently, penalties by inviting judges to take a tougher line with regulated professionals.

In a way, disciplinary sanctions are already sufficient in themselves, since they can lead to heavy fines, which are more or less bearable depending on the banking or financial institution, but above all can cause significant damage to the reputation of the institution concerned.

The anti-money laundering system thus set up, in compliance with international texts and European directives, seems to be rapidly fulfilling the task for which it was intended. In fact, the mechanisms that have been developed seem to completely lock down the financial sector, and it seems difficult today to use it to launder money.

What's more, although its implementation has been tricky, professionals seem to have gradually complied with it. Unfortunately, not everyone is so optimistic on the subject. For many, the French anti-money laundering system raises a number of questions.

B) <u>Questions raised by the French anti-money laundering system</u>

Despite all the work that has been done, there are still many critics of the anti-money laundering scheme. Among these, lawyers have long been the standard-bearers of opposition to the anti-money laundering scheme, considering it incompatible with French law. **(Section I) Nonetheless**, it is true that the system does raise some questions. **(Section II)**

<u>Section I: Strong opposition from lawyers to France's anti</u> money laundering measures

Although they are the professionals most concerned by the fight against money laundering, the banking and financial sector is not the only area of activity subject to the provisions. Under the terms of article L561-2 13°, "avocats au Conseil d'Etat et à la Cour de cassation, avocats, notaires, huissiers de justice, administrateurs judiciaires, mandataires judiciaires and commissaires-priseurs judiciaires" are also covered.

èmeAlthough surprising at first glance, this involvement of the regulated professions in the fight against money laundering actually stems from the European Anti-Money Laundering Directive of 2001, which noted in its 14ème recital that "*money launderers are increasingly tending to use non-financial professions. This trend is confirmed by the FATF's work on money laundering techniques and typologies*".

The Law of 11 February 2004 reforming the status of certain judicial and legal professions transposed the 2005 directive and introduced the regulated professions. It should be noted, however, that notaries have been subject to obligations relating to the fight against money laundering since *the Act of 2 July 1998 containing various provisions of an economic and financial nature*, which took into account the tendency of criminal organisations to launder their money through real estate companies, a favourite area of notarial activity.

Almost all of the provisions of the 2016 Order therefore apply to the regulated professions, although they do not apply to all of their activities. Article L561-3 of the CMF stipulates that these professionals are subject to the obligations of the scheme when they act in the name and on behalf of their client in any financial or real estate transaction or in a fiduciary capacity, or when they assist their client in the preparation or execution of various transactions listed in this article, including the purchase and sale of real estate or business assets or the incorporation, management or direction of companies.

II° of this same article also contains a special provision for lawyers, under which they are not subject to these obligations when their activity is related to legal proceedings, even if this activity concerns one of the transactions mentioned in I°. In this way, the law aims to protect the professional secrecy of lawyers as part of their duty to defend the interests of citizens.

Despite the many changes made by the legislator to the anti-money laundering provisions for the legal professions, discontent quickly mounted within the legal profession, which considered that the anti-money laundering directives, by subjecting professionals to an obligation to denounce money laundering, threatened the fundamental rights of citizens, the independence of the profession, professional secrecy and the confidentiality of correspondence between lawyers and their clients. By referring the matter to several courts[120] , the profession sought to challenge the validity of the application of the provisions of the Second Directive to lawyers. Although the Conseil d'Etat found that the measure complied with the principles of the profession and did not disproportionately infringe professional secrecy, it had to rule that the implementing decree of 26 June 2006 did not comply with the law.

Taking note of these decisions, the 2009 Order redefined the scope of the anti-money laundering obligations applicable to lawyers. One of the notable advances made by the Order concerns the reporting of suspicions. Adopting the solution adopted by the Conseil d'Etat in its decision of 10 April 2008, the Order stipulates, under Article L561-17 of the CMF, that lawyers must send their written report to the president of their

---

[120] The matter was referred to the Court of Justice of the European Communities (decision of 26 June 2007), the Belgian Constitutional Court (decision of 23 January 2008) and the Conseil d'Etat (decision of 10 April 2008).

bar association, who will be responsible for checking that the report meets the conditions for validity and for forwarding it to TRACFIN. Paragraph 2 of this article stipulates, however, that the French FIU must refuse to disclose the declaration if it considers that it has been sent in disregard of the cases provided for in Article L561-3 of the CMF and return it to the president of the bar association with which the lawyer is registered.

With these new provisions, the legislator wanted to prevent TRACFIN from interfering in the legal profession as much as possible in order to protect professional secrecy as effectively as possible.

The Order also provides for a derogation with regard to the disclosure of documents to TRACFIN for lawyers when they are not acting in a fiduciary capacity. Article L561-25 II stipulates that TRACFIN may not directly request a lawyer to disclose retained documents and must therefore submit its request to the President of the Bar Association with which the lawyer is registered. If this procedure is not followed, the lawyer has the right to oppose disclosure. In addition, both the lawyer and the President of the Bar are subject to the same confidentiality obligations as other persons subject to the law, with regard to the non-disclosure of the declaration to the client.

Lastly, article L561-18 of the CMF provides that lawyers and other liberal professions may not disclose information if they are seeking to dissuade their clients from committing illegal activities, as this is inherent to their activity.

The final specificity introduced by the 2009 Order for the legal profession concerns the supervisory role played by the President of the Bar, in the same way as the supervisory authorities. Article L561-28 III° of the CMF stipulates that if the President of the Bar discovers facts likely to be linked to money laundering during the performance of his supervisory role, he must immediately inform the Public Prosecutor at the Court of Appeal, who will then forward the report to TRACFIN.

However, the introduction of a specific regime for lawyers within the French anti-money laundering system has not won over practitioners. In 2011, only one suspicious transaction report was issued by lawyers, compared with 15,582 for banks, 1,069 for notaries and 17 for bailiffs over the same period[121] . It was against this backdrop that Patrick Michaud, a tax lawyer, decided to oppose the mechanism, considering it incompatible with professional secrecy and the presumption of client innocence.

It had already referred the matter to the Conseil d'Etat, where it had sought to challenge the legality of the Conseil National des Barreaux's regulation of 12 July 2007

---

[121] **TRACFIN Annual Activity Report 2011**

instituting the procedure for reporting suspicions and the duty of constant vigilance for the legal profession. In a ruling handed down on 23 July 2010, the Supreme Court dismissed the appeal on the grounds that the text did not excessively infringe professional secrecy or the confidentiality of exchanges with clients. In addition, it ruled that the measures in the legislation were legitimate, given the public interest in combating money laundering and the financing of terrorism.

Having failed to win his case before the Conseil d'Etat, the lawyer then decided to take his case to the European Court of Human Rights (ECHR) on the basis of the right to a fair trial (article 5 of the European Convention on Human Rights), the principle that there is "no punishment without law" (article 7) and the protection of privacy (article 8).

While invoking Articles 5 and 7 may be legitimate in view of the litigant's claims, invoking the right to protection of privacy seems more surprising. This was precisely the lawyer's strategy, since he based his argument on ECHR case law holding that the registered office and business premises of a company enjoy the same legal protection as that attached to the home[122] . In addition to this first case law, the ECHR also considered that the confidentiality of professional communications was just as guaranteed as communications taking place in a private context[123] .

Thus, on 6 December 2012, the ECHR handed down the landmark **_Michaud v France_** judgment rejecting the lawyer's application, on almost the same grounds as those of the Conseil d'Etat. The Court accepted that the obligation to report interfered with "private business life", but considered that this interference was provided for by law, as envisaged by Article 8(2) of the ECHR[124] , and also served a legitimate aim, namely the necessary fight against money laundering and the financing of terrorism.

Having regard to those considerations, the Court considers that, having regard to the purpose pursued by the contested measure, it does not constitute a disproportionate breach of lawyers' professional secrecy and of the confidentiality of exchanges with clients. That it is not disproportionate is confirmed by two points in the anti-money laundering provisions, namely :

- The obligation to declare only concerns advisory activities, which are far removed from the primary mission entrusted to lawyers. Furthermore, the law specifies that lawyers are not subject to this obligation when they are acting in the context of legal proceedings. In this way, the obligation to declare "_does_

---

122 **Case. Niemietz v. Germany,** 16 December 1992, _European Court of Human Rights_
123 **Case. Frérot v France,** 12 June 2007, _European Court of Human Rights_
124 CESDH stands for "European Convention for the Protection of Human Rights". Considered to be the legal basis guaranteeing human rights and fundamental freedoms at Community level.

not therefore affect the very essence of the task of defence, which is the basis of lawyers' professional secrecy"[125] .

- The introduction of a "protective filter" for professional secrecy by the fact that lawyers do not send their declarations directly to TRACFIN but through the President of the Bar Association with which they are registered. Consequently, the communication of confidential information to a professional subject to the same ethical rules and elected by his peers in no way undermines professional secrecy.

This decision put an end to a long polemic involving the entire profession. However, no one could have predicted how lawyers would react to the *Michaud v France ruling* at the end of 2012, given their total lack of interest in the anti-money laundering mechanism (from 2008 to 2011, TRACFIN had received only 6 declarations from lawyers).

The question thus remained delicate on another point, that of sanctions in the event of non-compliance with the anti-money laundering provisions. Since the power to impose sanctions in the legal profession lies with the relevant bar association, it was difficult to imagine this authority sanctioning a lawyer for non-compliance with an obligation rejected by the profession as a whole.

By now, the debate seems to have died down and no one is talking about the incompatibility between the duty to report suspicions and lawyers' professional secrecy. But then, have lawyers complied with these provisions?

The figures provided by the recent *TRACFIN 2017 activity report* published on 21 June 2018 show that not, since despite a "peak" in 2013 with a total of 6 declarations issued, none were made in 2017.

It therefore seems clear that the legal profession is still very reluctant to apply the French anti-money laundering provisions.

Section II: Questions raised by the anti-money laundering provisions

On the face of it, the picture that emerges today is rather optimistic, with the vast majority of countries having set up bodies to regulate and supervise banking and financial activities, and with these bodies cooperating closely with international or intergovernmental institutions while referring to their recommendations and opinions.

The French anti-money laundering system, transposed from the IIème and then the

---

[125] **L'obligation de déclaration de soupçon incombant aux avocats dans le cadre de la lutte contre le blanchiment ne porte pas une atteinte disproportionnée au secret professionnel,** 6 December 2012, *Press release by the Registrar of the Court*

IIIème European anti-money laundering directive, now seems to be well established. There is still a high level of legislation in this area and new texts are constantly being added to reinforce the provisions already in place, both against money laundering and against the financing of terrorism.

The *Act of 6 December 2013 on combating tax fraud and serious financial crime* is a perfect example of this, as it introduced a series of important new provisions to strengthen the system, such as the possibility for anti-corruption associations to bring civil actions, the increase in penalties for tax fraud offences[126] , and the introduction of a penalty of general confiscation of assets if a legal entity is convicted of money laundering.

Similarly, with regard to the financing of terrorism, *the Act of 13 November 2014 strengthening the provisions relating to the fight against terrorism* adds to Article L562-2 of the CMF that the Minister of the Interior may now decide to freeze, for a renewable period of 6 months, assets, funds and financial instruments deposited with banking and financial institutions belonging to persons who commit or attempt to commit terrorist acts. This power, which originally belonged to the Minister for the Economy, can now be used jointly with the Minister for the Interior when the situation so requires.

However, in addition to this generally positive state of affairs, certain points may legitimately raise questions, particularly in terms of legal compliance. These provisions do not necessarily always reconcile well with other principles established by common law.

Among these is one of the fundamental principles that bankers must respect in the course of their business: the duty of non-interference. What remains of this basic principle of banking law?

Unfortunately, the obligations imposed by the anti-money laundering provisions are so far-reaching that the banker is obliged to monitor and even 'track' his customer's activities. If this is the case, could the banker be held liable for failing to comply with this duty of non-interference?

Another question concerns the right to an account under article L312-1 of the CMF.

This right to an account allows individuals or legal entities domiciled in France to apply to the Banque de France if they are repeatedly refused an account by credit institutions. Following this request, the applicant will be able to have a bank account opened in the establishment of their choice designated by the Banque de France, and this establishment will not be able to refuse them this time.

---

[126] Under the 2013 Act, the penalty for aggravated tax fraud is seven years' imprisonment and a fine of €2,000,000.

The question arising from this principle of general law with regard to anti-money laundering legislation concerns its compatibility with article L561-8 of the CMF, which requires the business relationship to be terminated if it is impossible to obtain information about the customer or the nature of the planned relationship. How will credit institutions react, torn between their obligation to open an account for the customer following the Banque de France's designation and their duty of vigilance, non-compliance with which is likely to be sanctioned by the ACPR?

Similarly, one can only wonder about the legal consequences of this obligation to unilaterally terminate the business relationship, especially in the case provided for by L561-9 II° of the CMF where the professional, having considered the risk of money laundering to be low, has already entered into this relationship with the customer.

In the light of the current case law of the Cour de Cassation (French Supreme Court), it would appear to be advisable for the trial judge to ensure that the professional has properly fulfilled his obligation of due diligence. The Court of Cassation therefore recommends a case-by-case assessment based on the intensity of the existing risk and not on the due diligence obligation provided for *in abstracto* by the Monetary and Financial Code. This means that those subject to the law can go even further in fulfilling their duty of vigilance, which could justify calling into question other principles specific to the banking profession.

It will nevertheless be up to the courts to deal with and fill these gaps in the legislation. The other question that may be raised concerns the perverse effect that the profusion of legislation and the extension of the scope of application in the fight against money laundering could have.

Indeed, the extension of the system, initially introduced by the 2009 Order, to tax fraud offences means that banking and financial institutions are now obliged to identify such fraud and report it to TRACFIN, with many authors fearing that the French FIU will become "a formidable tool in the fight against tax fraud, to the detriment of its original purpose".[127] In addition, given the tougher stance taken by the supervisory authorities towards professionals in the banking and financial sector, the latter will only be encouraged to increase their reporting of suspicions in order to benefit from the exemption from civil and criminal liability that comes with reporting. As well as optimising the fight against money laundering, all of these points could lead to TRACFIN becoming clogged up and its initial objective being redirected towards the hunt for tax evaders.

Apart from these factors, which obscure the effectiveness of the French anti-money

---

[127] **L'extension du champ de la déclaration de soupçon et ses conséquences,** *Chantal Cutajar, 2009,* Revue de droit bancaire et financier

laundering system, the fight against money laundering continues. The public authorities remain on the lookout, scrutinising and studying the slightest techniques likely to be used by money launderers to carry out their activities.

It was through this ongoing effort that the authorities had very quickly assessed the potential danger posed by electronic currencies, well before the adoption of the Vème anti-money laundering directive in 2018.

In a June 2014 report drawn up by the "virtual currencies" working group led by TRACFIN[128] , it was pointed out that these electronic currencies were characterised by the involvement of unregulated players, a lack of transparency and the notion of extraterritoriality, the latter contributing greatly to the development of new techniques for money launderers. This was the case with the *Silk Road* website, which specialised in the sale of illicit products, mainly narcotics, and for which all transactions were paid for in Bitcoins. The site was finally shut down by US law enforcement agencies on 2 October 2013.

Even today, TRACFIN continues to study new avenues for improvement, particularly through the case studies presented in its annual activity reports, which detail and explain concrete and new money laundering situations.

It is therefore highly likely that the French anti-money laundering system will continue to evolve.

The war thus declared on criminal organisations, terrorists and, more recently, fraudsters seems to be gradually gathering momentum, encompassing a wide range of professions, each more varied than the last, likely to be implicated in the crimes of money launderers. Although there are still a number of gaps in the system, it is now beginning to be put in place, making the days of the Compliance departments of credit and financial institutions a joy to behold.

The balance sheet is therefore fairly positive, but we will have to be careful that the necessary fight against money laundering, through its many measures to monitor customer activities, does not gradually lead to a reduction in individual freedoms, even though, as is often the case, it is because of the excesses of some that everyone is constrained.

Bibliography :

KOUTOUZIS Michel, THONY Jean-François. **Le Blanchiment**. Collection " Que sais- je ? Presses Universitaires de France, 2005

KOPP Pierre. **Analyse économique comparée de la lutte anti-blanchiment : droit continental versus Common-Law,** 2006

---

[128] **L'encadrement des monnaies virtuelles - Recommandations visant à prévenir leur usage à des fins frauduleuses ou de blanchiment,** June 2014, *"virtual currencies" working group.*

*POWIS Robert E. **The Money Launderers: lessons from the drug wars,** 1992*
*HOUNNONGANDJI Francis. **Ordinary stories of fraud,** Eyrolles, 2011*
*CHAPPEZJean. **La lutte internationale contre le blanchiment des capitaux d'origine illicite et le financement du terrorisme,** Annuaire français de droit international, 2003.*

Public documents :

*Cour des Comptes. **TRACFIN and the fight against money laundering,** Annual Public Report, February 2012*
*Autorité de Contrôle Prudentiel et de Résolution. **Bilan des missions de contrôle sur place sur le respect des obligations de LCB-FT dans le domaine de la gestion de fortune pour les secteurs de la banque et de l'assurance,** Report of February 2012*
*Autorité des Marchés Financiers. **Guidelines of the Autorité des Marchés Financiers clarifying certain provisions of the General Regulation on the prevention of money laundering and terrorist financing,** 15 March 2010.*
*Autorité des Marchés Financiers. **Lignes directrices sur la notion de personnes politiquement exposées en matière de lutte contre le blanchiment des capitaux et le financement du terrorisme (Guidelines on the concept of politically exposed persons in the fight against money laundering and terrorist financing),** position-recommendation of 13 February 2013.*
*TRACFIN, **Annual activity report 2011***
*TRACFIN, **Annual Activity Report 2017***
*Virtual currencies working group. **The supervision of virtual currencies: Recommendations aimed at preventing their use for fraudulent purposes or money laundering,** June 2014.*

Periodicals :

*MANOUK Vonny. **Genesis of the money laundering process,** Revue internationale de Criminologie et de Police Technique et Scientifique (RICPTS)*
*DEFFERARD Fabrice. **The metamorphoses of French anti-money laundering legislation,** Gazette du Palais 2009*
*CONTE Philippe. **Aspect pénal des obligations de vigilance tendant à prévenir le blanchiment,** JCP G 2005.*
*Press release from the Registrar of the Court. **L'obligation de déclaration de soupçon incombant aux avocats dans le cadre de la lutte contre le blanchiment ne porte pas une atteinte disproportionnée au secret professionnel,** 6 December 2012*

CUTAJAR Chantal. **L'extension du champ de la déclaration de soupçon et ses conséquences,** Revue de droit bancaire et financier, 2009

Le Point. ***The fight against money laundering*: lawyers put up resistance,** 20 September 2012

Le Figaro. **Fraud and money laundering: nearly 30,000 reports received by Tracfin in 2013,** 4 March 2014

L'Express. **Financial intelligence: TRACFIN's activity jumped 30% in 2014,** 16 April 2015

EurActiv, **La directive anti-blanchiment vidée de son ambition de transparence,** 18 December 2014

Webography :

Légifrance, the public service for disseminating the law: http: //www. legifrance. gouv.fr

Europa, access to European Union law: http://eur-lex.europa.eu

European Court of Human Rights website: https://www. echr.coe.int

Financial Action Task Force (FATF) website: http://www.fatf-gafi.org

Autorité de Contrôle Prudentiel et de Résolution (ACPR) website: http://acpr.banque-france.fr

Autorité des Marchés Financiers (AMF) website: http://www.amf- france.org

TRACFIN website: http://www.economie.gouv.fr/tracfin

Conseil National des Barreaux website: http://cnb.avocat.fr

Robert Schuman Foundation website: http://www.robert-schuman.eu/fr